The Handy LONDON MAP & GUIDE

C000226134

Published by Bensons Mapguides

✉ info@bensonsmapguides.co.uk
🌐 bensonsmaps.co.uk
☎ 020 8830 9090

© Fernando Benito & Pedro Benito, 2014
Edition 18 (2014)

ABOUT THIS GUIDE

STAR RATINGS FOR SIGHTSEEING
All places, monuments, museums and attractions listed in this guide are of some interest, but the most significant sights are given star ratings in order to indicate their relative importance for visitors to London. The star ratings are defined as follows:

✳✳✳✳✳ Exceptional
✳✳✳✳ - *worth a journey*

✳✳✳ Very Interesting
✳✳ - *worth a detour*

✳ Interesting

ADMISSION CHARGES
The entrance prices quoted in this guide apply to adults only and are *subject to change*. There are usually reduced prices available for children, concessions and occasionally for groups. Some places of interest permit free entry to young children when accompanied by an adult.

OPENING HOURS
It should be noted that the opening hours given in this guide are *subject to change* and may not apply on public holidays. The *last admission* time is usually earlier than the *closing* time. Please check in advance with the particular establishment.

■ **BRITISH MUSEUM** ✯✯✯✯✯   22 A3

The national collections of archaeology, prints and drawings, coins and medals and ethnography. This museum, the greatest and biggest of its kind in the world, was founded in 1753 and occupies a neoclassical building begun in 1823 to the designs of Sir Robert Smirke.

Its incomparable collections of antiquities include treasures such as the *Portland Vase*, the *Rossetta Stone*, the *Parthenon sculptures* (Elgin Marbles) and the *Egyptian mummies*.

The huge **Great Court** is an impressive glass-roofed atrium with exhibition spaces, lecture theatres, educational facilities, shops and cafés. In its centre, the spectacular **Reading Room** was originally the Museum's library department and is currently a space for major exhibitions.
Open daily 10:00-17:30 (Fri until 20:30); admission free; ☎ *020-7323 8299;* Ⓦ *britishmuseum.org;* ⊖ *Russell Sq., Tottenham Court Road, Holborn.*

■ **BUCKINGHAM PALACE** ✯✯✯✯   37 C1

The principal residence of the sovereign since the accession to the throne of Queen Victoria in 1837. When the Queen is in residence, the Royal Standard is flown from the flagpole. *The State Rooms are open in Aug and Sep daily from 09:30 (last admission 17:15 in Aug and 16:15 in Sep); adult £19.75;* ☎ *020-7766 7300;* Ⓦ *royalcollection.org.uk*

The biggest attraction of the palace is the colourful ceremony of **Changing the Guard**✯✯✯✯ which takes place usually daily at 11:30 (alternate days Aug to Mar), affairs of state and weather permitting. ⊖ *Green Park, St. James's Park, Victoria.*

■ **HOUSES OF PARLIAMENT** ✯✯✯✯   38 B1

A majestic building in the late Gothic style, known officially as the New Palace of Westminster, which stands on the site of the old royal Palace of Westminster (founded in the 11th century, rebuilt in the 13th and 14th century and burnt down in 1834).

Designed by Sir Charles Barry, assisted in the details by Augustus Pugin, and built between 1837 and 1888, it incorporates the crypt of St. Stephen's Chapel and Westminster Hall (two surviving parts of the medieval palace). The building occupies over 8 acres and, besides the House of Commons and the House of Lords, it contains offices, libraries, a dining hall and other rooms.

At the north end of the building stands London's most famous landmark: the majestic **Big Ben**✯✯✯, the name popularly given to the graceful 97m Elizabeth Tower, although it is actually the nickname of the Great Bell that strikes the hours and weighs over thirteen and a half tons.

At the southwest corner of the building stands the **Victoria Tower**✯ (1860) which houses the archive for parliamentary documents, some of which date back to 1497. At the west side of the building stands **Westminster Hall**✯✯✯ with a splendid **hammerbeam roof**✯✯✯ which is considered the finest of its kind in the world. Built in the 11th century and last rebuilt in the 14th century, it has witnessed the most famous state trials in English history.
Public access is restricted. When the House is in session, debates can be seen from the public gallery (queue at St. Stephen's Entrance). There are guided tours Sat all year and selected weekdays Aug-Oct; adult £25; ☎ *0844 847 1672 (bookings);* Ⓦ *parliament.uk;* ⊖ *Westminster.*

■ **NATIONAL GALLERY** ✯✯✯✯✯   30 A

Holding over 2,300 works, this is one of the world's greatest and most important galleries and probably the one that best covers all schools of Western European painting from the 13th to the 19th century. Each of the schools is represented by some exceptional works. *Open daily 10:00-18:00 (Fri until 21:00); admission free* ☎ *020-7747 2885;* Ⓦ *nationalgallery.org.uk* ⊖ *Charing Cross.*

■ **ST. PAUL'S CATHEDRAL** ✯✯✯✯✯   32 A

Sir Christopher Wren's masterpiece, the seat of the Bishop of London, was built (1675-1710) on the site of the old Gothic cathedral burnt down in the Great Fire of 1666. It is a beautiful Renaissance building dominated by the splendid dome (111m high), the largest in the world after St. Peter's in Rome.

The **interior** impresses by its amplitude and for the wealth of its ornamentation. See in particular the inner face of the great **dome**✯✯✯✯; the **monument** to Wellington (in the nave); the **monument** to Nelson (in the south transept); the wrought-iron **gates** by Tijou (Choir) and the **organ case** and beautiful choir **stalls** both carved by Grinling Gibbons and the **crypt**✯✯ containing more than 100 tombs including those of Nelson, Wellington and Wren.

CLIMB THE DOME: from the south aisle, a staircase *(259 steps)* leads to the **Whispering Gallery**, 30m above the floor of the cathedral. A further climb *(118 steps)* leads to the external **Stone Gallery** at the base of the dome. From here there are extensive **views**✯✯✯ of London. The last part of the climb, the hardest *(153 steps)*, brings you to the **Golden Gallery** at the foot of the lantern, 85.4m high, which offers impressive **views**✯✯✯ over London.
Open to sightseers 08:30-16:00 Mon-Sat only; adult £16.50; ☎ *020-7246 8357;* Ⓦ *stpauls.co.uk* ⊖ *St. Paul's, Mansion House.*

■ **SCIENCE MUSEUM** *See page 13.*

■ **TATE BRITAIN** ✯✯✯✯   38 A

The national gallery of British art showing works from 1500 to the present day. See works by Rubens, Hogarth, Blake, Constable, Bacon, Turner and very many more.

The magnificent Turner Collection, in the **Clore Gallery**, exhibits some of the 300 oil paintings nd over 19,000 drawings and watercolours that Turner left to the nation. *Open daily 10:00-18:00; admission free;* ☎ *020-7887 8888;* ⓦ *tate.org.uk;* ⊖ *Pimlico.*

■ TATE MODERN ★★★★ 32 A2

Britain's gallery of international modern and contemporary art is housed in the vast space of the former Bankside Power Station and is a hugely popular attraction. It displays the Tate Collection of international 20th century art and features major works by influential artists. Works are displayed in themed rooms. New 21st century art is also exhibited. *Open Sun-Thu 10:00-18:00, Fri-Sat 10:00-22:00; admission free;* ☎ *020-7887 8888;* ⓦ *tate.org.uk;* ⊖ *Southwark.*

■ TOWER OF LONDON ★★★★★ 33 D2

An imposing fortress by the Thames, which has been a royal residence, a state prison and nowadays is one of London's main tourist attractions, watched over by the famous Yeoman Warders who wear picturesque uniforms designed in the 16th century. The origins of the Tower date back to 1078 when William the Conqueror began building its oldest part, the White Tower. The walls and the rest were built at later stages.

The most important parts are: the **White Tower★★★★**, which contains a collection of arms and armour and, on the second floor, the **Chapel of St. John★★**, London's oldest church (1080); the **Crown Jewels★★★** kept in the Jewel House; the **Medieval Palace**, where King Edward I lived in the 13th century; the **site of the scaffold**, where the most noble heads rolled, including those of two of Henry VIII's wives, Anne Boleyn and Catherine Howard; the towers **Beauchamp, Wakefield** and **Bloody**; the **Traitors' Gate** through which the boats with provisions or prisoners once entered.

Open Mar-Oct, Tue-Sat 09:00-17:30 and Sun-Mon 10:00-17:30; Nov-Feb, Tue-Sat 09:00-16:30, Sun-Mon 10:00-16:30; last admission 30 minutes prior to closing; adult £20; ☎ *020-3166 6000;* ⓦ *hrp.org.uk/toweroflondon;* ⊖ *Tower Hill.*

■ VICTORIA & ALBERT MUSEUM ★★★★ 35 D2

Also known as *the V&A*, this is Britain's National Museum of Art and Design, founded in 1851 by Prince Albert, husband of Queen Victoria. The museum's collections hold some of the greatest decorative art treasures from around the world including Sculpture, Ceramics, Glass, Metalwork, Photography, Architecture, Fashion and Jewellery, Furniture and Furnishings.

The stunning **British Galleries** trace the story of British Design from Tudor through to Victorian times.

The V&A keeps the world's greatest collection of Constables and a magnificent Dress Collection, which shows the history of European costume and fashion from 1600 right up to the present day. *Open Sat-Thu 10:00-17:45, Fri 10:00-22:00; admission free;* ☎ *020-7942 2000;* ⓦ *vam.ac.uk;* ⊖ *South Kensington.*

■ WESTMINSTER ABBEY ★★★★★ 38 A1

The most important building to visit in London because of its architectural interest and more so because of its long association with British history. It has hosted every coronation from William the Conqueror in 1066 to Elizabeth II in 1953, excepting Edward V and Edward VIII, and is home to the Coronation Chair. The Abbey is also the final resting place for many monarchs including Edward I, Henry III, Henry V, Henry VII, Elizabeth I, Mary I and Mary Queen of Scots. In addition, thousands of eminent men and women are also buried or commemorated here.

Built in Gothic style by Henry III in the 13th century, the abbey has had important additions, such as Henry VII's Chapel in the 16th century and the twin towers in the 18th century. Of prime interest are: the tomb of the **Unknown Warrior**; the unique **Chapel of Henry VII★★★**; the **Chapel of St. Edward the Confessor★★**, containing the Shrine of the Saint (d.1066); and the **Poets' Corner★★** in which great poets and writers are buried or commemorated.

Open for sightseers Mon-Fri 09:30-16:30 (Wed until 19:00), Sat 09:30-14:30; last admission one hour before closing; adult £18, free for under-11s; ☎ *020-7222 5152;* ⓦ *westminster-abbey.org;* ⊖ *Westminster.*

OTHER PARTS OF THE ABBEY:

1 Great Cloisters ★ This area dates from the 13th and 14th century and was central to daily activity in the medieval monastery.

2 Chapter House ★★★ Built in the mid-13th century, this is a noble octagonal chamber with a central pier supporting the lofty vault.

3 Abbey Museum ★ A collection of funeral effigies of monarchs and other illustrious subjects in period attire. *Open daily 10:30-16:00.*

4 Dean's Yard A square flanked by a number of medieval monastic buildings.

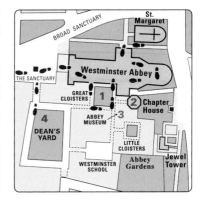

■ **ADMIRALTY ARCH** 30 A3

A massive curved triumphal arch designed by Aston Webb and built in 1910 as part of a national memorial to Queen Victoria. ⊖ *Charing Cross.*

■ **ALBERT MEMORIAL** ✱ 35 C1

This unique and opulent monument to Prince Albert (1819-61), the consort of Queen Victoria, was designed by Sir George Gilbert Scott (1872) and has been restored to its original splendour. *Guided tours Mar-Dec on first Sun of month at 14:00 and 15:00 (meet by the memorial on the side that faces the Royal Albert Hall); adult £7;* ☎ *020-7936 2568;* ⊖ *South Kensington.*

■ **BARBICAN CENTRE** ✱✱ 24 B3

This massive multi-arts centre has nine levels (four of which are underground) and includes the splendid **Barbican Hall**, the home of the London Symphony Orchestra; the **Barbican Theatre** and **The Pit** theatre; three cinemas, two art galleries, a library, restaurants, cafeterias and a tropical conservatory. *Open Mon-Sat 09:00-23:00 and Sun 10:00-23:00;* ⊖ *Barbican.*

■ **BEDFORD SQUARE** ✱ 22 A3

Built at the end of the 18th century, this is one of the most interesting squares in London and has survived with its Georgian houses quite unspoiled. ⊖ *Tottenham Court Road.*

■ **BELGRAVE SQUARE** 36 B1

The most majestic square to be seen in Belgravia, boasting on each side an exceptionally impressive range of buildings with houses on a palatial scale. ⊖ *Hyde Park Corner.*

■ **BERKELEY SQUARE** 29 C2

This large square was one of the most aristocratic and elegant in London and still retains its beautiful gardens with enormous plane trees, planted around 1790, and some fine period houses on the west side. ⊖ *Green Park.*

■ **BIG BEN** ✱✱✱ 38 B1

See HOUSES OF PARLIAMENT, page 2.

■ **BT TOWER** 21 D3

This famous London landmark is a part of the nation's telecommunications system. On completion in 1965, it was the tallest structure in central London (189m). *Not open to the public.*

■ **CENOTAPH** 30 B3

National memorial (1920) for all members of the British and Commonwealth forces who died in the two world wars and later conflicts. ⊖ *Westminster.*

■ **CHINATOWN** ✱ 30 A2

Filled with a great number of restaurants, the lively Chinese quarter of London centres on Gerrard Street with its exotic street furniture. ⊖ *Piccadilly Circus, Leicester Square.*

■ **CITY, THE** 32 B1

The City of London (usually referred to as "The City") occupies the area roughly equivalent to Norman London: about one square mile. It is governed by a corporation presided by the Lord Mayor (elected annually), 24 other Aldermen and 132 Common Councilmen. The City is one of the main financial centres of the world and has its own police force, the *City of London Police.*

■ **CITY HALL** 33 D3

This distinctive riverside building is the seat of the Mayor of London, the London Assembly and the offices of the staff of the Greater London Authority. Some parts of the building are open to the public and include an information desk, cafeteria and exhibition space. *Open Mon-Thu 08:30-18:00, Fri 08:30-17:30;* ☎ *020-7983 4000,* ⓦ *london.gov.uk;* ⊖ *London Bridge.*

■ **CLEOPATRA'S NEEDLE** 30 B2

This 18m high rose-pink granite obelisk was erected in Heliopolis in about 1475 B.C. and was given to the British in 1819 but was only brought to Britain and installed at its present site in 1878. ⊖ *Embankment.*

■ **COVENT GARDEN** ✱✱✱ 30 B2

In the centre of the square, designed by Inigo Jones in 1631, the market buildings that exist today were built in 1828-31 and housed the principal market for fruit and vegetables in London until 1974. After the market relocated, the buildings were refurbished and are now occupied by shops, restaurants, cafés and pubs. The whole area is hugely popular, not least because of the thriving tradition of street entertainment around the *Piazza.* ⊖ *Covent Garden.*

■ **CUTTY SARK** ✱ 44

Launched in 1869, the last surviving tea clipper was the greatest and fastest of her time. In 1885 she sailed from Australia to England in just 73 days. *Open daily 10:00-17:00; admission £13.50;* ☎ *020-8858 4422;* DLR *Cutty Sark,* ⇌ *Greenwich.*

■ **DOWNING STREET** 30 A3

Number 10 is the official residence of the Prime Minister. *Not open to the public;* ⊖ *Westminster.*

■ **DRAKE'S GOLDEN HINDE** ✱ 32 B2

Berthed in historic Southwark, this is a full-sized reconstruction of the Tudor warship in which Sir Francis Drake circumnavigated the world (1577-80). Launched in Devon in 1973, this replica has sailed over 140,000 miles - many more than the original. *Usually open daily 10:00-17:30, please telephone for details; adult £7;* ☎ *020-7403 0123;* ⊖ *London Bridge.*

■ **FORTNUM & MASON** ✱✱ 29 D2

This famous department store was founded in 1707 by Mr. Fortnum and Mr. Mason. Their effigies are seen slowly emerging next to the clock above the front door after the hourly chimes. The staff in the renowned food hall wear tail-coats (red at Christmas). ⊖ *Piccadilly Circus, Green Park.*

■ **GABRIEL'S WHARF** 31 D2

Set by the River Thames, this is a pleasant enclave of speciality shops, restaurants and bars. *Shops open Tue-Sun 11:00-18:00;* ⊖ *Waterloo.*

■ GEORGE INN ✳   32 B3

London's only remaining galleried inn dates from 1676 and originally flanked three sides of the courtyard. It is mentioned in Dickens' novel *Little Dorrit*. **⊖** *London Bridge.*

■ GRAY'S INN ✳   23 C3

One of the four Inns of Court within which tranquil surroundings lawyers have worked since the 14th century. In the **hall** (1560, rebuilt 1951), Shakespeare's *The Comedy of Errors* was first staged in 1594. **⊖** *Chancery Lane.*

■ GROSVENOR SQUARE ✳   28 B2

This large and elegant square has been associated with the United States since John Adams, the "first minister plenipotentiary" and later President, occupied No. 9 (1785-8). On the west side the U. S. Embassy dominates and on the north side of the gardens is a memorial to Franklin D. Roosevelt. **⊖** *Bond Street.*

■ GUILDHALL ✳✳✳   32 B1

The seat of the Corporation that has governed the City since the first Mayor was installed here in 1189. The present Guildhall's foundation was laid around 1411, from which remains the medieval wall of the Great Hall, the porch and the crypt. The majestic **Great Hall** is used for municipal and public meetings, banquets and ceremonies. *Open May-Sep daily 10:00-16:30, Oct-Apr Mon-Sat 10:00-16:30 (except during functions); admission free;* **☎** *020-7606 3030;* **⊖** *Bank, Moorgate, St. Paul's.*

■ HARRODS ✳✳✳   36 A1

The largest and best known of London stores, Harrods started in 1849 as a simple grocery shop. The present building of terracotta brick dates from 1905 and covers five acres. With more than 200 departments, this luxurious store prides itself in being able to provide its customers with almost anything. **⊖** *Knightsbridge.*

■ HAY'S GALLERIA ✳   33 C3

Once the River Thames's most famous wharf, now a pleasant venue comprising shops, restaurants, cafés and a craft market under a spectacular glass and steel roof. **⊖** *London Bridge.*

■ HORSE GUARDS ✳   30 A3

This 18th century building is the backdrop for the daily spectacle of pageantry. On the Whitehall side, two mounted troopers are posted daily 10:00-16:00 (guard changes hourly). The ceremony of **Changing the Guard**✳ takes place *Mon-Sat at 11:00 and Sun at 10:00; the dismounted inspection is daily at 16:00.* **⊖** *Charing Cross, Westminster.*

■ JEWEL TOWER ✳   38 B1

This 14th century building is the only remaining domestic part of the medieval Palace of Westminster and once held the King's valuables. *Open Apr-Sep daily 10:00-18:00, Oct daily10:00-17:00, Nov-Mar Sat-Sun10:00-16:00; adult £4;* **☎** *020-7222 2219;* **⊖** *Westminster.*

■ LEADENHALL MARKET   33 C1

Dating from 1881, this structure has very elaborate arcades and was once a marketplace for meat, fish, game and provisions. The site was the heart of Roman London. *Open Mon-Fri.*

■ LEICESTER SQUARE ✳✳   30 A2

This pedestrianised square sits right in the heart of London's bustling nightlife. Located on its south side is a clocktower building in which one finds the official **TKTS half-price theatre ticket booth**, where discounted and half-price theatre tickets can be bought for same day performances *(open Mon-Sat 10:00-19:00, Sun 11:00-16:30).* **⊖** *Leicester Square.*

■ LIBERTY ✳   29 D1

This famous and stylish department store boasts an interesting mock Tudor façade, which was built in 1924 utilising timber salvaged from two Royal Navy ships. **⊖** *Oxford Circus.*

■ LINCOLN'S INN ✳✳   31 C1

One of the four Inns of Court founded in the 14th century. Of prime interest are: the charming **New Square** surrounded on three sides by 17th century buildings now occupied mainly by solicitors; the **Chapel** (1620-23) raised on vaulted arches; **The Old Hall** which dates back to 1491 and the **Old Buildings** dating mainly from the 16th century. *Open Mon-Fri;* **⊖** *Chancery Lane.*

■ LLOYD'S ✳   33 C1

This is the world's leading insurance market. Originating in the 1680s, Lloyd's is a society of underwriters who accept insurance risks for their personal profit or loss. The unusual building is Grade I listed and was opened in 1986. *Not open to the public;* **⊖** *Bank, Monument.*

■ LONDON BRIDGE EXPERIENCE   32 B2

This attraction is located in gloomy vaults below London Bridge and presents some of its history along with **The London Tombs**, an exhibition with a dark, scary theme. *Open Sun-Fri 10:00-17:00, Sat 10:00-18:00; adult £24;* **☎** *0800 0434 666;* **⊖** *London Bridge.*

■ LONDON DUNGEON   30 B3

A macabre exhibition that simulates the horrors of grisly murder, execution, torture and disease throughout British history. Displays include *Guy Fawkes - Gunpowder Plot, Jack the Ripper* and *Sweeney Todd. Open Fri-Wed from 10:00, Thu from 11:00 (closing times vary); adult £25.20;* **☎** *0871 423 2240;* **⊖** *Waterloo, Westminster.*

■ LONDON EYE ✳✳✳   30 B3

This hugely popular observation wheel is 135m tall and offers superb, far-reaching **panoramic views**✳✳✳ across the capital's skyline. With 32 fully enclosed capsules, each accommodating up to 25 people, it operates on a continuous rotation taking around 30 minutes to complete a full 360 degrees. *Open daily usually from 10:00 until 20:30 or 21:30; adult £20.95 (advance discounted booking is very strongly recommended);* **☎** *0870 990 8883;* **Ⓦ** *londoneye.com;* **⊖** *Westminster, Waterloo.*

■ LONDON ZOO ★★★   20 B1
Founded in 1826, the world's oldest zoo is a popular family attraction which promotes wildlife conservation. *Open daily 10:00-17:30 (until 16:00 in winter); adult £26; ☎ 0844 225 1826; ⊖ Baker Street (then 274 bus) or Camden Town (then 274 bus or on foot).*

■ LORD'S CRICKET GROUND   19 C1
The famous home of Middlesex County Cricket Club. The guided tour includes viewings of the Long Room, dressing rooms, MCC Museum, grandstand and media centre. *Daily guided tours, please telephone for further details; adult £18; ☎ 020-7616 8595; ⊛ lords.org; ⊖ St. John's Wood.*

■ MADAME TUSSAUDS ★★★   20 B3
This famous and hugely popular waxworks ex-hibition originated in 1802 and has been on its present site since 1884. Life-size wax models of famous and infamous world figures, past and present, are displayed in themed areas. *Open daily 09:30-17:30; adult £30; ☎ 0871 894 3000; ⊛ madametussauds.com; ⊖ Baker Street.*

■ MARBLE ARCH   28 A1
Designed by John Nash in 1828, inspired by the Arch of Constantine in Rome, it was placed outside Buckingham Palace and moved in 1851 to its present site, previously known as Tyburn, where public executions were carried out in the six hundred years up to 1783. *⊖ Marble Arch.*

■ MAYFAIR   29 C2
The elegant district that is bounded by Oxford Street, Regent Street, Piccadilly and Park Lane. A fair held each May from 1688 until the mid-18th century gave its name to the area, which was mainly developed in the first half of the 18th century. This upmarket residential area is dotted with luxury hotels, restaurants, some embassies, private galleries, offices and elegant shops.

■ MILLENNIUM BRIDGE   32 A2
Described as a "blade of light", this sleek walk-way spans the Thames and links St. Paul's Cathedral on the north side of the river to the Tate Modern on the south bank. *⊖ St. Paul's.*

■ MONUMENT, THE ★   33 C2
Sir Christopher Wren's colossal doric column surmounted by a flaming urn was erected in 1671-77. It commemorates the Great Fire of London, which started on 2nd September 1666 at a bakery in nearby Pudding Lane some 61 metres away from the column's location (equal to the column's height). A spiralling climb of 311 steps leads to a platform that affords panoramic **views*** of the metropolis. *Open daily Apr-Sep 09:30-18:00, Oct-Mar 09:30-17:30; adult £4; ☎ 020-7626 2717; ⊖ Monument.*

■ NELSON'S COLUMN ★   30 A2
See TRAFALGAR SQUARE, page 8.

■ OLD BAILEY   32 A1
Officially known as *Central Criminal Court*, it is the principal court for cases remitted from all over England and Wales. The current building

was opened in 1907 on the site of the old court and Newgate Prison, in front of which public executions used to take place from 1783 to 1868. *The public may be admitted when the courts are sitting, Mon-Fri 10:00-13:00 and 14:00-17:00; admission free; ⊖ St. Paul's.*

■ OLD OPERATING THEATRE   33 C3
The operating theatre of St. Thomas's Hospital from 1821-62 (discovered and restored in 1956) which was used as Florence Nightingale's School of Nursing from 1860. *Open daily 10:30-17:00; adult £6.50; ☎ 020-7188 2679; ⊖ London Bridge.*

■ PICCADILLY CIRCUS ★★★   29 D2
Flanked by huge electronic advertisements, this world-famous crossroads is always busy with crowds of people seeking out the diverse entertainments on offer in the West End. It is adorned by a fountain topped by the famous statue known as **Eros** (the Greek god of Love) which has become a symbol of London and a popular rendezvous. In fact, rather than Eros the statue was intended to portray the Angel of Christian Charity. *⊖ Piccadilly Circus.*

■ RIPLEY'S BELIEVE IT OR NOT!   29 D2
With over 500 weird and unusual exhibits on five floors, this attraction aims to amaze and entertain. *Open daily 10:00-00.00, last admission 90 minutes before closing; adult £26.95; ☎ 020 3238 0022. ⊖ Piccadilly Circus.*

■ ROYAL ALBERT HALL ★   35 C1
Built (1867-71) in the form of an oval amphithe-atre 83m by 72.5m, with an upper frieze in terracotta around the full length of the exterior wall that depicts the triumphs of Arts and Sciences. The venue has a capacity of 5,250 and is the setting for a diverse programme of per-formances, including the famous annual *Prom* concerts. *⊖ South Kensington.*

■ ROYAL COURTS OF JUSTICE ★   31 C1
The principal courts in the country for hearing civil cases (The High Court of Justice), and for criminal and civil appeals (The Court of Appeal) occupy an impressive Gothic building (1882). *When the courts sit (Oct-Jul) the public may be admitted to the galleries, Mon-Fri, 10:30-13:00 and 14:00-16:30; admission free; ⊖ Temple.*

■ ROYAL EXCHANGE ★   33 C1
First built in 1565-67 as a meeting place for inter-national commerce, it was made "Royal" by Elizabeth I in 1570. The present classical building was opened by Queen Victoria in 1844 and is now a shopping arcade showcasing luxury retailers and restaurants. *⊖ Bank.*

■ ROYAL FESTIVAL HALL ★   31 C3
The Hall was opened in 1951 as part of the *Festival of Britain* and is now a world-class performance venue. As well as the auditorium there are spacious **foyers** *(open daily 10:00-23:00)* offering seating, a bar, a café, a restaurant, a shop, live music and frequent art exhibitions. *⊖ Embankment, Waterloo.*

ROYAL MEWS * — 37 C1

This is where the Queen's horses and carriages can be viewed. See the new Diamond Jubilee State Coach (2014) and the Gold State Coach which was built in 1762 and has been used at every coronation since. *Open Feb-Mar Mon-Sat 10:00-16:00, Apr-Oct daily 10:00-17:00 and Nov Mon-Sat 10:00-16:00 (N.B. dates and times are subject to change); adult £8.75; ☎ 020-7766 7302;* ⊖ *Victoria.*

ROYAL NAVAL COLLEGE, OLD ** — 44

An impressive baroque ensemble that was planned mainly by Sir Christopher Wren in 1695. It stands upon the site of the royal palace where Henry VIII, Mary I and Elizabeth I were born. It first served as a Royal Hospital to aid seamen and their dependants. Then, from 1873 to 1998, it was used as a naval training centre for officers. See the **Painted Hall** with murals by Sir James Thornhill and the wonderfully ornate **Chapel**. *Open daily 10:00-17:00 (Chapel open from 12:30 in Sun); admission free; ☎ 020-8269 4799;* ⓦ *ornc.org;* DLR *Cutty Sark,* ⇌ *Greenwich.*

ROYAL OBSERVATORY GREENWICH ** — 44

Founded by Charles II in 1675 as a centre for navigational research, it has been the home of Greenwich Mean Time since 1884. The zero meridian of longitude passes through here, and millions of visitors have been photographed straddling the line that divides East and West of our planet. It houses Britain's largest refracting telescope plus a unique collection of historic timepieces and astronomical instruments. In addition, there is a state-of-the-art **planetarium**, the only one in London. *Open daily 10:00-17:00; adult £7 (additional charge for planetarium); ☎ 020-8858 4422;* ⓦ *rmg.co.uk/royal-observatory;* ⇌ *Greenwich,* DLR *Cutty Sark.*

ROYAL OPERA HOUSE * — 30 B1

The London home of international opera and ballet. The present theatre, the third on this site (1732 and 1809), was built in 1856-8 by E. M. Barry and was refurbished in 1999. The graceful **Floral Hall** is usually open to the public daily 10:00-15:30. *There are regular backstage guided tours (please telephone to obtain details); ☎ 020-7304 4000;* ⓦ *roh.org.uk;* ⊖ *Covent Garden.*

ST. JAMES'S SQUARE * — 29 D2

This fine square, laid out after 1660, retained the favour of the aristocracy until recently. Most of the houses have been rebuilt at one time or another. ⊖ *Piccadilly Circus.*

ST. KATHARINE DOCKS ** — 33 D2

These once busy docks have been converted into a successful commercial and leisure complex, with visiting yachts, Thames barges and other sailing crafts creating the atmosphere of a coastal holiday village. ⊖ *Tower Hill.*

SEA LIFE LONDON AQUARIUM — 30 B3

One of Europe's largest displays of global aquatic life featuring thousands of living specimens. Housed within historic County Hall, its vast tanks allow visitors a close look at the fascinating inhabitants of the various natural environments recreated within. *Open daily 10:00-19:00, last admission 18:00; adult £21.60; ☎ 0871 663 1678;* ⊖ *Westminster, Waterloo.*

SHAKESPEARE'S GLOBE THEATRE & EXHIBITION ** — 32 A2

The original Globe, burnt down in 1613, has been rebuilt with the utmost attention to detail and incorporated into an educational, cultural and entertainment complex. *Open daily (please telephone for opening times which are subject to variation); adult £13.50; ☎ 020-7902 1500;* ⓦ *shakespearesglobe.com;* ⊖ *Mansion House.*

SHARD, THE * — 33 C3

This iconic building is the tallest (310m) in Western Europe and has redefined the London skyline. On floors 68, 69 and 72, **The View from The Shard*** affords an unrivalled look at the cityscape. *Open daily Apr-Oct 10:00-22:00, Nov-Mar Sun-Wed 10:00-19:00 and Thu-Sat 10:00-22:00; adult £29.95 (advanced booking is strongly recommended); ☎ 0844 499 7111;* ⓦ *theviewfromtheshard.com;* ⊖ *London Bridge.*

SHEPHERD MARKET — 29 C3

A charming village-like quarter formed by narrow streets and alleys with shops, pubs, restaurants and cafés. The popular annual *May Fair*, which gave its name to the district, used to be held here. ⊖ *Green Park.*

SOHO — 29 D1

This famous district is bordered by Oxford Street, Charing Cross Road, Leicester Square, Piccadilly Circus and Regent Street. It is composed of a labyrinth of small streets, mostly from the 17th and 18th century, with its main road, **Shaftesbury Avenue**, built at the end of the 19th century and famous for its theatres (Shaftesbury, Apollo, Gielgud, Lyric, Palace and Queen's). Since the 17th century Soho has had a very cosmopolitan population and nowadays it is a gastronomic centre, where the most important of the world's cuisines are represented. The area is also renowned for its strip clubs and sex shops, although these are now in decline.

SPEAKERS' CORNER — 28 A2

An open space just inside Hyde Park, where orators - some brilliant, some uninspired - gather on Sundays to deliver their speeches on political, religious and other issues, providing a free and picturesque diversion. ⊖ *Marble Arch.*

STAPLE INN * — 23 C3

From the 15th century to 1884, Staple Inn was one of London's nine Inns of Chancery, where law students spent their first year. The unique **façade***, made up of half-timbered houses built in the 17th century (restored), gives an idea of how the City looked before the Great Fire of 1666. ⊖ *Chancery Lane.*

■ **TEMPLE, THE** ★★★   31 D1
A vast enclosure occupied until 1312 by the
military order of the Knights Templars (founded
in 1119 in Jerusalem). This enclave of Georgian
buildings and gardens, amongst which lawyers
have their chambers, is an oasis of tranquillity.
It includes the **Middle Temple** and the **Inner
Temple** which are two of the Four Inns of Court;
the legal societies which have the exclusive
right of admitting persons to practice law at the
English bar. ⊖ *Temple.*

IN AND AROUND THE TEMPLE:

1 The George This fine timbered inn dates
from 1723 when it was opened as one of the
fashionable coffee houses.

2 Twinings The tea and coffee merchant, with
a golden lion and two Chinamen above the door,
was opened in 1706 as *Tom's Coffee House.*

3 Child & Co. (Now part of the Royal Bank of
Scotland). Presumed to be the oldest bank in
London, it has been at No. 1 Fleet Street since 1673
(rebuilt in 1879), and is the original of Tellson's
Bank in Dickens' *A Tale of Two Cities.*

4 Temple Bar Memorial Located in the middle
of the road, this monument from 1880 marks
the boundary of the City of Westminster and
the City of London where Temple Bar once
stood (it now stands near to St. Paul's Cathedral).

5 Middle Temple Hall ★ In this magnificent
hall Shakespeare's *Twelfth Night* was first
performed on 2nd February 1602.

6 Temple Church ★ This fine and interesting
church has a round nave, completed in 1185,
based on the Church of the Holy Sepulchre in
Jerusalem and a rectangular Gothic style chancel
which was added in 1220-40. *Usually open to*

Map labels:
Royal Courts of Justice — St. Dunstan in the West — Gateways — FLEET ST. — 8 Ye Olde Cock Tavern — SERJEANTS INN — Temple Bar Memorial — 4 — 7 — 2 — 3 Child & Co. — Twinings — The George — 6 — Temple Church — ESSEX ST. — MILFORD LA. — 5 — Middle Temple Hall — The Temple — EMBANKMENT — VICTORIA — HQS Wellington — HMS President

visitors Mon-Fri 11:00-13:00 and 14:00-16:0[
Sun 14:00-16:00; adult £4, free for under-18s.

7 Inner Temple Gateway (1610-11), a beauti[
half-timbered building which contains a fi[
17th century room on the first floor: **Princ[
Henry's Room** *(currently closed to the public*

8 Ye Olde Cock Tavern This famous C[
tavern is the oldest in Fleet Street and w[
frequented by Pepys, Dickens and Tennyso[

■ **TOWER BRIDGE** ★★★   33 [
Opened in 1894, this world-famous landmark h[
twin Gothic towers linked near the top by t[
fully-glazed walkways 42m above the river. *T[
Tower Bridge Exhibition* brings this uniq[
bridge's history to life with interactive displa[
and videos. Visitors can enjoy splendid **view**[
the Thames from the walkways and enter t[
Victorian **Engine Rooms** to see the origin[
steam engines that once powered the bridge lif[
Open daily Oct-Mar 09:30-17:30, Apr-Sep 10:0[
18:00 (last admission 30 minutes before closin[
adult £9; ☎ *020-7403 3761;* ⊖ *Tower Hill.*

■ **TRAFALGAR SQUARE** ★★★   30 A[
The most famous square in London, comme[
orates Admiral Nelson's victory over the flee[
of France and Spain at Cape Trafalgar along t[
Spanish coast in 1805. It is a grand ensemb[
adorned with statues, fountains and the 50[
high **Nelson's Column**★. This granite mon[
ment to Nelson is surmounted by the statue [
the Admiral (erected in 1843). The pedestal [
the base is adorned with four bronze reliefs ca[
from captured French guns. The four coloss[
lions were added in 1867. ⊖ *Charing Cross.*

■ **TROCADERO**   30 A[
An entertainment complex with a mix of sho[
places to eat, a cinema and arcade amusemen[
Open daily 10:00 until late; ⊖ *Piccadilly Circ[*

■ **VAULT, THE**   29 C[
Beneath the Hard Rock Cafe Shop, this is [
showcase for the best pieces of rock memorabi[
from Hard Rock's collection. *Open daily 11:3[*
21:00; admission free; ⊖ *Hyde Park Corner.*

■ **VINOPOLIS**   32 [
An exhibition and dining complex dedicated [
the appreciation of wine and spirits where visito[
can take a tour and enjoy tastings. *Open W[*
18:00-21:30, Thu-Fri 14:00-22:00, Sat 12:0[
21:30, Sun 12:00-18:00 (last admission up to th[
hours before closing); adult from £27; ☎ *02[*
7940 8300; ⊖ *London Bridge.*

■ **WELLINGTON ARCH**   28 [
Decimus Burton's design was finished in 18[
and surmounted in 1912 by a huge bronze qu[
riga with a figure of *Peace.* There are fine **view**[
from its balconies. *Open daily Apr-Sep 10:00-18:[*
Oct 10:00-17:00, Nov-Mar 10:00-16:00; adu[
£4.20; ☎ *020-7930 2726;* ⊖ *Hyde Park Corn[*

■ **WESTMINSTER HALL** ★★★   38 [
See HOUSES OF PARLIAMENT, page 2.

HOUSES & PALACES 9

■ **APSLEY HOUSE** ★★ 28 B3
This was the first Duke of Wellington's home from 1817 until his death in 1852. The restored interior reflects its original splendour and contains works of art collected by the victor of Waterloo and his descendants. *Open Apr-Oct Wed-Sun 11:00-17:00, Nov-Mar Sat-Sun 11:00-16:00; adult £6.90;* ☎ *020-7499 5676;* ✪ *Hyde Park Corner.*

■ **BANQUETING HOUSE** ★★ 30 B3
The only important building to survive from the great Palace of Whitehall which was the sovereign's metropolitan residence from 1530 until it was burnt down in 1698. This masterpiece by Inigo Jones was completed in 1622 and has spacious and well proportioned **Banqueting Hall** which was enriched in 1635 with Rubens' splendid **ceiling paintings**★★★. *Open daily 10:00-17:00 (except when closed for ceremonies); adult £6, free for under-16s;* ☎ *020-3166 6000;* ✪ *Embankment, Westminster.*

■ **BUCKINGHAM PALACE** *See page 2.*

■ **CLARENCE HOUSE** ★ 29 D3
The official London residence of the Prince of Wales, the Duchess of Cornwall, Prince William and Prince Harry. From 1953 to 2002 it was the home of Queen Elizabeth The Queen Mother. All tours are guided and view the rooms used for official engagements where much of Queen Elizabeth's famous art collections are on display. *Open in Aug Mon-Fri 10:00-16:00 and Sat-Sun 10:00-17:30; adult £9.50;* ☎ *020-7766 7303;* ✪ *Green Park.*

■ **DR. JOHNSON'S HOUSE** 31 D1
A typical late 17th century house in which Dr. Samuel Johnson lived (1749-59) while compiling his famous dictionary. *Open Mon-Sat 11:00-17:30 (17:00 in winter); adult £4.50;* ☎ *020-353 3745;* ✪ *Chancery Lane, Blackfriars.*

■ **KENSINGTON PALACE** ★★★ 26 A3
Queen Victoria lived in this modest palace from her birth until her accession to the throne in 1837 and it was the home of Diana, Princess of Wales. Highlights of a visit include: **Queen Victoria's bedroom**; the **King's State Apartments** including the beautiful **King's Gallery** where hangs a stunning collection of Old Masters. *Open daily Mar-Oct 10:00-18:00, Nov-Feb 10:00-17:00; adult £15, free for under-16s;* ☎ *020-3166 6000;* ✪ *Queensway, High Street Kensington.*

■ **LAMBETH PALACE** 38 B2
This site has been the official residence of the Archbishops of Canterbury for around 800 years. Its entrance is a Tudor gatehouse (15th century). *Not normally open to the public;* ✪ *Westminster, Lambeth North.*

■ **LANCASTER HOUSE** 29 D3
A beautiful mansion where Queen Victoria often visited her friend, the Duchess of Sutherland. *Not open to the public;* ✪ *Green Park.*

■ **MANSION HOUSE** ★ 32 B1
Completed in 1752, the official residence of the Lord Mayor of London is a classical building with a Corinthian portico. ✪ *Bank.*

■ **QUEEN'S HOUSE** ★★ 44
Elegant Palladian villa designed by Inigo Jones (1616) and completed in 1638 for Charles I's queen Henrietta Maria, who called it her "house of delights". The royal apartments have been restored to their former splendour and the house is now a gallery space for the National Maritime Museum's rich art collections. *Open daily 10:00-17:00; admission free;* ☎ *020-8858 4422;* **DLR** *Cutty Sark,* ≈ *Greenwich.*

■ **ROYAL HOSPITAL CHELSEA** ★★ 36 B3
Designed by Christopher Wren, this home for veteran and disabled soldiers, founded in 1682 by Charles II, was inspired by Louis XIV's *Hôtel des Invalides* in Paris. The "Chelsea Pensioners" wear distinctive blue or scarlet uniforms, the latter dating back to the 18th century.
In the central part of the building are the **Chapel** and the panelled **Great Hall** (dining hall) where the Duke of Wellington lay in state in 1852. *Open Mon-Sat 10:00-12:00 and 14:00-16:00, Sun 14:00-16:00; admission free;* ✪ *Sloane Square.*

■ **ST. JAMES'S PALACE** ★ 29 D3
Built by Henry VIII in 1532-36, this mansion became the sovereign's official residence in London after the Whitehall Palace fire in 1698 and until Queen Victoria moved to Buckingham Palace in 1837. In fact foreign ambassadors are still accredited to "the Court of St. James's".
See the picturesque 16th century **Gatehouse** on the north side which has octagonal towers and original linenfold-panelled doors. On the east side, **Friary Court** is the assembly point for the Old Guard of the Foot Guards that marches to the *Changing of the Guard* ceremony at Buckingham Palace. Opposite Friary Court is the **Queen's Chapel** which was designed by Inigo Jones and was England's first classical church (1623-7). *St. James's Palace is not open to the public;* ✪ *Green Park.*

■ **SOMERSET HOUSE** ★ 31 C2
A majestic building of 1777-86 designed in classical style by Sir William Chambers, with an impressive frontage to the Thames. The wide **River Terrace** and the expansive **Courtyard** are open to the public, the latter being also a venue for events and performances. In addition, the building houses **Embankment Galleries** and the revered **Courtauld Gallery**★★★ *(see pages 11-12). Admission free to Courtyard and Terrace;* ☎ *020-7845 4600;* ✪ *Temple.*

■ **SPENCER HOUSE** ★ 29 D3
The ancestral home of the late Diana, Princess of Wales was built in 1756-66 for the first Earl Spencer. *Open Sun (except during Jan and Aug); all tours are guided and run at regular intervals from 10:30 until 16:45 (last tour); adult £12;* ☎ *020-7499 8620;* ✪ *Green Park.*

■ **ALL HALLOWS-BY-THE-TOWER** ✱ 33 D2
This church dates from the 7th century and has been rebuilt several times. It is well worth visiting, as is the crypt. Be sure to see the beautiful carved font cover and the 7th century Anglo-Saxon arch. *Open Mon-Fri 08:00-17:00, Sat-Sun 10:00-17:00;* ☎ *020-7481 2928;* ✆ *Tower Hill.*

■ **BROMPTON ORATORY** ✱ 35 D1
A Roman Catholic church in the Italian baroque style, consecrated in 1884. The interior, notable for its sumptuous decoration, for the beauty of its design and for its proportions, contains works of art brought from Italy. *Open daily 06:30-20:00;* ☎ *020-7808 0900;* ✆ *South Kensington.*

■ **ST. BARTHOLOMEW THE GREAT** ✱ 24 A3
London's oldest parish church is also one of the most interesting. It belonged to an Augustinian priory founded in 1123 by Rahere, a courtier of Henry I. The 12th century choir and the 13th century transept constitute the present church which is a fine example of the Romanesque style in its oldest parts. *Open Mon-Fri 08:30-17:00 (16:00 in winter), Sat 10:30-16:00, Sun 08:30-20:00; adult £4;* ☎ *020-7600 0440;* ✆ *Barbican.*

■ **ST. BRIDE'S** ✱ 31 D1
Wren's tallest church (69m) was built in 1703 and is possibly his most beautiful. Often dubbed "the wedding cake church" due to the shape of its steeple✱, a baker named Mr. Rich made a fortune selling cakes resembling it. In the crypt there is an illustrated record of two thousand years of the church and its community, set amid the remains of a Roman building and seven churches. *Usually open Mon-Fri 09:00-18:00, Sun 10:00-18:30;* ☎ *020-7427 0133;* ✆ *Blackfriars.*

■ **ST. CLEMENT DANES** ✱ 31 C1
The central church of the Royal Air Force presents a beautiful steeple added by James Gibbs in 1719. The harmonious interior has more than 800 reproductions of the badges of the squadrons and units of the RAF and the Commonwealth, embedded in the floor. As the famous "Oranges and Lemons" church, the bells ring merrily at 09:00, 12:00, 15:00, 18:00 and 21:00. *Open daily 09:00-16:00;* ☎ *020-7242 8282;* ✆ *Temple.*

■ **ST. ETHELDREDA'S** ✱ 23 D3
A gothic jewel of 1290 with a crypt of 1251. Situated in a private cul-de-sac lined by 18th century houses, it is all that survives of the Bishop of Ely's mansion. *Open Mon-Sat 08:00-17:00, Sun 08:00-12:30;* ✆ *Chancery Lane, Farringdon.*

■ **ST. GILES CRIPPLEGATE** ✱ 24 B3
A church with 900 years of history, rebuilt in 1545-50 and restored in 1959 after bombs had destroyed the interior in 1940. The poet John Milton is buried here (see engraved floor stone close to the pulpit), and Oliver Cromwell was wed here in 1620. *Open Mon-Fri 11:00-16:00;* ☎ *020-7638 1997;* ✆ *Barbican, Moorgate, St. Paul's.*

■ **ST. HELEN BISHOPSGATE** ✱ 33 C1
This is known as "the Westminster Abbey of the City" due to the number and interest of its monuments. *Open Mon-Fri 09:30-12:30 (call for afternoon opening times); enter via church office (south side);* ☎ *020-7283 2231;* ✆ *Bank, Aldgate, Liverpool Street.*

■ **ST. JAMES, PICCADILLY** ✱ 29 D2
With a wonderful interior, this is one of only two Wren churches to be found outside the City (built 1676-84, restored 1947-54). *Open daily 08:30-18:30;* ☎ *020-7734 4511;* ✆ *Piccadilly Circus.*

■ **ST. MARGARET'S** ✱ 38 A1
The present church, the third on the site, was consecrated in 1523 and has been known as "the parish church of the House of Commons" since 1614. The unique **East Window** commemorates the marriage of King Henry VIII to his first wife, Catherine of Aragon. *Usually open for visitors Mon-Fri 09:30-15:30, Sat 09:30-13:30, Sun 14:00-16:30;* ☎ *020-7654 4840.*

■ **ST. MARTIN-IN-THE-FIELDS** ✱ 30 B2
This masterpiece by James Gibbs (1722-6) replaced a royal parish church erected for Henry VIII in 1544. It is a beautiful example of baroque architecture, featuring an elegant spire and portico. It is a popular lunchtime and evening concert venue. The crypt contains a café, gallery, bookshop and brass-rubbing centre. *Open Mon-Fri from 08:30, Sat 09:30-18:00, Sun 15:30-17:00;* ☎ *020-7766 1100;* ✆ *Charing Cross.*

■ **ST. MARY-LE-BOW** ✱ 32 B1
Christopher Wren's famous church (built 1670-80) replaced the 11th century one which was lost in the Great Fire of 1666 except for the surviving Norman **crypt**, built on arches (or bows) of stone. The steeple✱ (66m high), is among Wren's finest achievements and houses the famous **Bow Bells** within which sound true Londoners, or "Cockneys", are said to be born. *Open Mon-Wed 07:30-18:00, Thu 07:30-18:30, Fri 07:30-16:00;* ☎ *020-7248 5139;* ✆ *St. Paul's, Bank.*

■ **ST. PAUL, COVENT GARDEN** ✱ 30 B2
Known as the Actors' Church, it was built by Inigo Jones in 1631-3 and rebuilt after a fire in 1798. The great Tuscan portico that overlooks the square is all that survives of Jones's church. The beautiful interior has memorials to Noël Coward, Charlie Chaplin, Vivien Leigh and many others. *Open Mon-Fri 08:30-17:00, Sun 09:00-13:00;* ☎ *020-7836 5221;* ✆ *Covent Garden.*

■ **ST. PAUL'S CATHEDRAL** See page 2.

■ **ST. STEPHEN WALBROOK** ✱ 32 B1
This masterpiece by Sir Christopher Wren has a simple exterior that contrasts with its sumptuous and perfectly proportioned interior. It is thought that the beautiful **dome**✱ may have served as a model for St. Paul's Cathedral. *Open Mon-Fri 10:00-16:00;* ☎ *020-7626 9000;* ✆ *Bank, Cannon Street.*

■ **SOUTHWARK CATHEDRAL** ✶✶✶ 32 B3
There has been a church on this site for over
one thousand years and this one is amongst the
oldest and most beautiful Gothic churches in
London. The majestic interior contains countless
interesting monuments, such as the memorial
to William Shakespeare, whose brother Edmund
is buried here. John Harvard, the founder of
Harvard University, was baptized here (1607)
and the **Harvard Chapel** is dedicated to his
memory. *Open daily 10:00-17:00; voluntary admission fee;* ☎ *020-7367 6700;* ⊖ *London Bridge.*

■ **TEMPLE CHURCH** ✶ 31 D1
See TEMPLE, THE; page 8.

■ **WESLEY'S CHAPEL & HOUSE** 25 C2
The Chapel has been the mother church of
Methodism since 1778 when it was opened by
the founder John Wesley, who lived in the adjacent house and is buried in the graveyard behind
the Chapel. *House, Chapel and crypt museum
are open Mon-Sat 10:00-16:00, Sun 12:30-13:45;
admission free;* ☎ *020-7253 2262;* ⊖ *Old Street.*

■ **WESTMINSTER CATHEDRAL** ✶✶ 37 D2
This is the largest and most important Roman
Catholic church in Great Britain and is the seat
of the Archbishop of Westminster. Built in 1895-
1903, it is an imposing structure in an early
Christian Byzantine style presenting an original
exterior with alternate bands of red brick and
Portland stone. The unfinished interior, which
gives the impression of vastness and fine proportions, is adorned by fine marbles and modern
mosaics. *Open daily 07:00-19:00.*
Ascending the 83m campanile by lift, one can
enjoy an extensive **view**✶ across West London.
Open daily 09:30-17:00; adult £5; ☎ *020-7798
9055;* ⊖ *Victoria.*

■ **BANK OF ENGLAND MUSEUM** ✶ 32 B1
This interesting museum uses material from
the Bank's collections to tell the history of the
Bank since its foundation by Royal Charter in
1694. The displays include an interactive video
exhibition which explains the Bank's role today.
*Open all year Mon-Fri 10:00-17:00; admission
free;* ☎ *020-7601 5545;* ⊖ *Bank.*

■ **BANKSIDE GALLERY** 32 A2
The home of the Royal Watercolour Society and
the Royal Society of Painter-Printmakers. *Open
during exhibitions daily 11:00-18:00; admission
free;* ☎ *020-7928 7521;* ⊖ *Blackfriars.*

■ **BRITISH LIBRARY** 22 A1
   EXHIBITION GALLERIES ✶✶
There are three galleries open to the public of
which the most important is the **Treasures
Gallery** which displays some 200 of the Library's
most famous items including *Magna Carta*, the
Lindisfarne Gospels, the *Gutenberg Bible* and the
*First Folio Shakespeare. Open Mon-Fri 09:30-
18:00 (Tue until 20:00), Sat 09:30-17:00 and
Sun 11:00-17:00; admission free;* ☎ *020-7412
7676;* ⊖ *King's Cross St. Pancras, Euston.*

■ **BRITISH MUSEUM** *See page 2.*

■ **CARTOON MUSEUM** 30 A1
A celebration of the best of British cartoons,
caricature and comic art from the 18th century
onwards. *Open Mon-Sat 10:30-17:30, Sun 12:00-
17:30; adult £7, free for under-18s;* ☎ *020-7580
8155;* ⊖ *Tottenham Court Road, Holborn.*

■ **CHARLES DICKENS MUSEUM** ✶ 23 C2
The home of Charles Dickens during 1837-9,
where the celebrated author completed *The
Pickwick Papers* and wrote *Oliver Twist* and
*Nicholas Nickleby. Open daily 10:00-17:00; adult
£8;* ☎ *020-7405 2127;* ⊖ *Russell Square.*

■ **CHURCHILL WAR ROOMS** ✶✶ 38 A1
An engaging exhibition dedicated to the life and
achievements of the iconic leader Sir Winston
Churchill. The setting for this tribute is the
underground command post where Churchill,
his War Cabinet and Chiefs of Staff of Britain's
armed forces sheltered during enemy bombing
raids on London in the Second World War.
Visitors can see the Cabinet Room, the Map
Room and the Prime Minister's room. *Open
daily 09:30-18:00; adult £17.50, free for under-
16s;* ☎ *020-7930 6961;* ⊖ *Westminster.*

■ **CLINK PRISON MUSEUM** 32 B2
On the site of the original Clink Prison, this
exhibition traces its history and displays
restraining and torture devices. *Open Jul-Sep
daily 10:00-21:00, Oct-Jun Mon-Fri 10:00-18:00
and Sat-Sun 10:00-19:30; adult £7.50;* ☎ *020-
7403 0900;* ⊖ *London Bridge.*

■ **CLOCKMAKERS' MUSEUM** 32 B1
Situated within the Guildhall Library, this
wonderful collection displays timepieces dating
mostly from c.1600 to c.1850. *Open Mon-Sat
09:30-16:45; admission free;* ☎ *020-7332 1868;*
⊖ *Bank, St. Paul's.*

■ **COURTAULD GALLERY** ✶✶✶ 31 C2
A superb set of private collections that includes
the outstanding Impressionist and Post-
Impressionist paintings bequeathed by *Samuel
Courtauld*, as well as Renaissance, Baroque and
20th century works. *Open daily 10:00-18:00;
adult £6 (£3 on Mon), free for under-18s;* ☎
020-7848 2526; ⊖ *Temple, Covent Garden.*

■ **DESIGN MUSEUM** 33 D3
This museum is celebrates and explores all
aspects of modern design evolution. *Open daily
10:00-17.45; adult £12.40;* ☎ *020-7940 8790;*

⊖ *Tower Hill, London Bridge.*

■ EMBANKMENT GALLERIES 31 C2
This venue hosts temporary exhibitions of art, design, fashion, architecture and photography. *Open during exhibitions daily 10:00-18:00; admission charge;* ☎ 020-7845 4600; ⊖ *Temple.*

■ FASHION & TEXTILE MUSEUM 33 C3
This centre showcases contemporary fashion, textile and jewellery design in a series of changing exhibitions. *Open during exhibitions Tue-Sat 11:00-18:00 (Thu until 20:00), Sun 11:00-17:00; adult £8.80, free for under-12s;* ☎ 020-7407 8664; ⊖ *London Bridge.*

■ FLORENCE NIGHTINGALE 39 C1
MUSEUM
This museum celebrates Florence Nightingale's work to elevate the standards of hospitals and nursing. *Open daily 10:00-17:00; adult £7.80;* ☎020-7620 0374; ⊖ *Waterloo, Westminster.*

■ GARDEN MUSEUM 38 B2
This museum occupies the former church of St. Mary-at-Lambeth. The churchyard has been planted as a 17th century garden with species originally introduced by the great plant-hunters John Tradescant the Elder and the Younger. Their magnificent tomb is found here next to Admiral Bligh's (of *Mutiny on the Bounty* fame). *Open Sun-Fri 10:30-17:00, Sat 10:30-16:00 (not first Mon of month); adult £7.50, free for under-16s;* ☎ 020-7401 8865; ⊖ *Westminster, Lambeth North.*

■ GEFFRYE MUSEUM 25 D1
Set in charming Georgian Almhouses, this museum contains a fine collection of furniture and decorative art from 1600 to the present day. *Open Tue-Sun 10:00-17:00; admission free;* ☎ 020-7739 9893; ⊖ *Hoxton.*

■ GUARDS MUSEUM 37 D1
Within the grounds of the Wellington Barracks, this museum presents the history of the five Foot Guards regiments (Grenadiers, Coldstreams, Scots, Irish and Welsh) which extends over more than 350 years. *Open daily (except Christmas period) 10:00-16:00, last admission 15:30; adult £5, free for under-17s;* ☎ 020-7414 3428; ⊖ *St. James's Park.*

■ GUILDHALL ART GALLERY 32 B1
This gallery exhibits some of the City's extensive collection and houses the preserved remains of London's **Roman Amphitheatre**. *Open Mon-Sat 10:00-17:00, Sun 12:00-16:00 (occasionally closed for civic functions); admission free;* ☎ 020-7332 3700; ⊖ *Bank, St. Paul's, Moorgate.*

■ HANDEL HOUSE MUSEUM 29 C1
The home of the composer G. F. Handel, from 1723 until his death in 1759, has been restored to fine Georgian style and includes an exhibition about his life and works. *Open Tue-Sat 10:00-18:00 (Thu until 20:00), Sun 12:00-18:00; adult £6.50, free for under-16s on Sat-Sun;* ☎ 020-7495 1685; ⊖ *Bond Street.*

■ HAYWARD GALLERY 31 C
A centre holding exhibitions encompassing a forms of visual arts. *Open Tue-Sun from 10:0(, Mon from 12:00; admission charge varies;* ☎ 020-7960 4200; ⊖ *Waterloo, Embankment.*

■ HMS BELFAST ✶ 33 C
The last surviving Royal Navy big gun ship, thi cruiser was launched in 1938, and is now floating museum. *Open daily Mar-Oct 10:0(18:00, Nov-Feb 10:00-17:00; last admission on hour before closing; adult £15.50, free for unde 16s;* ☎ 020-7940 6300; ⊖ *London Bridge.*

■ HOUSEHOLD CAVALRY MUSEUM 30 C
Located within historic Horse Guards (see pa(5), this unique living museum offers a "behin(the-scenes" look at the work involved in meetin the regiment's ceremonial and operation; duties. *Open daily Apr-Oct 10:00-18:00, No(Mar 10:00-17:00; adult £7;* ☎ 020-7930 307(⊖ *Charing Cross, Westminster.*

■ ICA (Institute of Contemporary Arts) 30 A
This respected cultural centre includes tw(galleries, two cinemas and a theatre. *Art galleri(open during exhibitions Tue-Sun 11:00-18:0 (Thu until 21:00);* ☎ 020-7930 364; ⓦ ica.org.uk; ⊖ *Charing Cross, Piccadilly Circu*

■ IMPERIAL WAR MUSEUM ✶✶✶ 39 D
Illustrates all aspects of the wars that hav involved British and Commonwealth arme forces since 1914. Notable exhibits include th *Holocaust Exhibition, A Family in Wartime an Secret War. Open daily 10:00-18:00; admissio free;* ☎ 020-7416 5000; ⓦ *iwm.org.uk;* ⊖ *Lambeth North.*

■ LONDON FILM MUSEUM 30 B
This space holds exhibitions relating to film making. *Open Sun-Fri 10:00-18:00, Sat 10:0(19:00; adult £14.50;* ☎ 020-7836 4913; ⊖ *Covent Garden.*

■ LONDON TRANSPORT 30 B
MUSEUM ✶✶
The fascinating story of travel, people and th growth of London itself told through a super collection of transport memorabilia and vehicle spanning over 200 years. There are hands-o exhibits, videos and touchscreen displays. *Ope Sat-Thu 10:00-18:00, Fri 11:00-18:00; adult £1 (unlimited admission for a 12 month period, free for under-18s;* ☎ 020-7379 6344; ⊖ *Cove(Garden.*

■ MUSEUM OF LONDON ✶✶✶ 24 A
Discover London's fascinating story fro(prehistoric times onwards. The displays featu(interactive exhibits and archaeological artefact costumes, paintings and more. Highligh(include the spectacular **Galleries of Moder London** and the splendid Lord Mayor's Coac (1757) which is used at the annual Lord Mayor Show. *Open daily 10:00-18:00; admission fre(* ☎ 020-7001 9844; ⊖ *St. Paul's, Moorgate.*

■ NATIONAL ARMY MUSEUM ✶✶ 36 A3
Presents the fascinating history of the armies of Britain since the raising of the Yeomen of the Guard by Henry VII in 1485. *Closed for major redevelopment until 2016;* ⊖ *Sloane Square.*

■ NATIONAL GALLERY *See page 2.*

■ NATIONAL MARITIME 44
MUSEUM ✶✶✶
A celebration of Britain's seafaring heritage from Tudor times to the present. Visitors can see some of the finest items in the museum's collection within historic buildings which were formerly a school for the children of seamen. *Open daily 10:00-17:00; admission free;* ☎ *020-8858 4422;* DLR *Cutty Sark,* ⇌ *Greenwich.*

■ NATIONAL PORTRAIT 30 A2
GALLERY ✶✶✶
Displays portraits of the most eminent persons in British history from the Tudors to the present. Founded in 1856, the collection now comprises more than 10,000 portraits of which only about a third is on view. *Open daily 10:00-18:00 (Thu and Fri until 21:00); admission free;* ☎ *020-7306 0055;* ⊖ *Charing Cross, Leicester Square.*

■ NATURAL HISTORY 35 C2
MUSEUM ✶✶✶✶
The largest and most important natural history collection in the world is held in this stunning museum. Especially popular areas include the fascinating dinosaur exhibits, the *Creepy-crawlies* section and the *Human Biology Gallery.* The **Darwin Centre** gives an intriguing insight into scientific work currently underway on site. *Open daily 10:00-17:50; admission free;* ☎ *020-7942 5000;* Ⓦ *nhm.ac.uk;* ⊖ *South Kensington.*

■ PHOTOGRAPHERS' GALLERY 29 D1
London's largest public gallery dedicated to photography, showing both emerging and established talent. *Open Mon-Sat 10:00-18:00 (Thu until 20:00) and Sun 11:30-18:00; admission free;* ☎ *020-7087 9300;* ⊖ *Oxford Circus.*

■ QUEEN'S GALLERY ✶✶ 37 C1
This gallery holds temporary exhibitions of works from the splendid royal art collections. *Open daily 10:00-17:30; adult £9.25;* ☎ *020-7766 7301;* ⊖ *Victoria, St. James's Park.*

■ ROYAL ACADEMY OF ARTS ✶✶✶ 29 D2
Set within the elegant Burlington House (18th century), the society was founded in 1768 with the aim of fomenting the arts. It is renowned for its international loan exhibitions and its **Summer Exhibition** of submissions by living artists. The **Fine Rooms** *(free guided tours, see website for details)* show key works from the Academy's own great collection. *Exhibitions open Sat-Thu 10:00-18:00, Fri 10:00-22:00; admission fee varies;* ☎ *020-7300 8000;* Ⓦ *royalacademy.org.uk;* ⊖ *Piccadilly Circus, Green Park.*

■ ROYAL ACADEMY 20 B2
OF MUSIC MUSEUM
The displays include fine classical instruments and original manuscripts by great composers. *Open Mon-Fri 11:30-17:30, Sat 12:00-16:00; admission free;* ☎ *020-7873 7373;* ⊖ *Baker Street.*

■ SAATCHI GALLERY 36 A3
Located just off King's Road, within the grandiose Duke of York's Headquarters, this gallery shows temporary and curated contemporary art exhibitions. *Open daily 10:00-18:00; admission free;* Ⓦ *saatchigallery.com;* ⊖ *Sloane Square.*

■ SCIENCE MUSEUM ✶✶✶✶ 35 C1
The largest of its kind in the world, it has over 15,000 different exhibits, covering almost every imaginable sector of science, technology, industry and medicine. Its collections include over 2,000 interactive exhibits that allow visitors to explore and discover science and technology for themselves. The impressive **Wellcome Wing** has a suite of changing exhibitions and a 450-seat *IMAX* cinema (showing 3D science films). *Open daily 10:00-18:00; admission free (admission fees apply for IMAX, simulators and some special exhibitions);* ☎ *020 7942 4000;* Ⓦ *sciencemuseum.org.uk;* ⊖ *South Kensington.*

■ SERPENTINE GALLERY 27 C3
& SACKLER GALLERY 27 D3
Revered venues for exhibitions of all forms of modern and contemporary art and culture. *During exhibitions open Tue-Sun 10:00-18:00; admission free;* ☎ *020-7402 6075;* ⊖ *Lancaster Gate.*

■ SHERLOCK HOLMES MUSEUM 20 A2
Set in a period terrace house in Baker Street, this is a tribute to the fictional detective and his exploits as portrayed in the novels of Sir Arthur Conan Doyle. *Open daily 09:30-18:00; adult £10;* ☎ *020-7224 3688;* ⊖ *Baker Street.*

■ SIR JOHN SOANE'S MUSEUM ✶✶ 31 C1
Works of art and antiquities collected by the notable architect Sir John Soane (d. 1837) are shown in the house which he left to the nation with the condition that it be kept unaltered. The interesting collection has paintings, antiquities, architectural drawings, books, sculptures and furniture. *Open Tue-Sat 10:00-17:00; admission free;* ☎ *020-7405 2107;* ⊖ *Holborn.*

■ TATE BRITAIN *See page 2.*

■ TATE MODERN *See page 3.*

■ VICTORIA & ALBERT MUS. *See page 3.*

■ WALLACE COLLECTION ✶✶✶ 28 B1
This most elegant and original museum is situated on the north side of the beautiful Manchester Square. It is especially rich in 17th and 18th century French art, and has paintings, sculptures, furniture, porcelain, European and Oriental arms and armours. *Open daily 10:00-17:00; admission free;* ☎ *020-7563 9500;* ⊖ *Bond Street.*

■ WHITECHAPEL GALLERY Outside 33 D1
The modern and contemporary art exhibitions held here are often of great interest. *Open Tue-Sun 11:00-18:00 (Thu until 21:00); admission normally free;* ☎ *020-7522 7888;* ⊖ *Aldgate East.*

Main Shopping Areas

■ **BOND STREET** ✦✦✦   29 C2
This comprises two parts: *Old Bond Street*, built c.1686, and *New Bond Street*, c.1720. It is flanked by elegant shops specialising in all things luxurious including respected names such as: *Asprey*, for gold, silver and jewellery; *Burberry*, for upmarket clothing and accessories; and *Sotheby's*, the famous art auctioneers.

■ **CARNABY STREET**   29 D1
World-famous in the 1960s as the centre of London's fashion scene, this area has enjoyed a revival with the presence of a number of flagship fashion stores and alternative boutiques.

■ **COVENT GARDEN** ✦✦✦   30 B1/2
A lively, cosmopolitan shopping district with markets, boutiques, specialist shops and an abundance of cafés, bars and restaurants. Its focal point is the *Piazza* and the former vegetable market.

■ **JERMYN STREET**   29 D2
Well known for its shirtmakers but two particular shops should not be missed: **Paxton & Whitfield** at No. 93 selling a great variety of cheeses since it was founded in 1797; secondly, **Floris** the perfumers at No. 89 since 1730.

■ **KENSINGTON HIGH STREET**   34 A1
A popular shopping area offering a good mixture of larger stores and a great selection of trendy clothes shops and boutiques.

■ **KING'S ROAD** ✦   36 A3
This 1960s legend, the backbone of Chelsea, has developed into a very popular shopping street. The notable department store *Peter Jones* is at the junction with Sloane Square.

■ **KNIGHTSBRIDGE** ✦✦✦   36 A1
This is a very exclusive area that includes Beauchamp Place and parts of Knightsbridge, Sloane Street and Brompton Road. Goods of the highest quality are offered in luxury stores such as *Harrods* and *Harvey Nichols*.

■ **OXFORD STREET** ✦✦✦   28 B1-29 D1
London's most popular shopping street, particularly the section stretching from Marble Arch to Oxford Circus, with large department stores such as: *Selfridges*, London's second largest store with an impressive quantity and variety of household and fashion goods; *John Lewis*, with merchandise for the home and family; the principal branch of *Marks & Spencer*, with clothes, accessories and homeware; *Debenhams*, with various well-stocked departments; and also *House of Fraser*, selling a wide range of quality goods.

■ **PICCADILLY** ✦✦   29 D2
One of London's most imposing streets with luxury hotels and elegant shops. Here one finds the department store *Fortnum & Mason* with its renowned food hall and the beautiful *Princes Arcade*, *Piccadilly Arcade* and **Burlington Arcade**✦✦, a covered passageway built in 1819, with attractive shop windows that are synonymous with elegance and refinement.

■ **REGENT STREET** ✦✦✦   29 D1/2
Laid out in the early 19th century by John Nash it maintains an air of distinction and is world known for the elegance and high quality of it shops, most notably: *Liberty*, a department store (just off Regent Street) especially famous fo its printed fabrics; *Austin Reed*, a fashion store with quality menswear; *Burberry*, contemporary and traditional high quality British clothing *Jaeger*, with its exclusively designed Englis clothes; and *Hamleys*, the renowned toy store established in Regent Street since 1906.

Popular Markets

The following is a selection of the most popula markets in the capital:

■ **BERWICK STREET**   29 D
A lively, traditional market mainly fruit, vegeta bles and household goods, it originates from the 18th century. *Open Mon-Sat.*

■ **BOROUGH MARKET** ✦   32 B:
This award-winning fine foods market is a ver popular shopping destination. *Open Wed-Thi 10:00-17:00, Fri 10:00-18:00, Sat 08:00-17:00*

■ **CAMDEN MARKETS** ✦   See map belov
Camden's markets opened in 1974 and now ex tend along Chalk Farm Road to Camden Tow Underground station.
Camden Lock Market, where it all began, i one of the best known and busiest markets in London for crafts, antiques, clothes, accessorie and more; *open daily 10:00-18:00, very popula at weekends.*
Stables Market sells antiques, curios, collecta bles, clothing and more; *open daily from 10:00*
Camden Market mainly offers new and pre owned clothes; *open daily 10:00-17:30.*

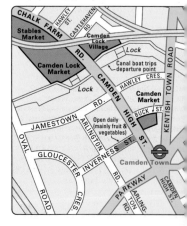

Camden Lock Village offers hot food, clothes, novelties and gifts; *open daily 10:00-20:30.*

■ **CAMDEN PASSAGE**   Outside **23 D1**
An enclave of small shops and stalls offering antiques, prints, books, jewellery and other collectables. *Markets open Wed from 07:00, Sat from 08:00;* ● *Angel.*

■ **JUBILEE MARKET**   **30 B2**
An indoor market held daily: antiques *(Mon 05:00-16:00)*; general goods *(Tue-Fri 09:30-18:30)*; arts and crafts *(Sat-Sun 09:30-17:30)*.

■ **LEATHER LANE**   **23 D3**
A busy lunchtime market with a variety of consumer goods. *Open Mon-Fri 10:00-14:30.*

■ **OLD SPITALFIELDS MARKET** ✳   **25 D3**
A popular market that has a diverse range. *Stalls open Mon-Fri 10:00-17:00, Sat 11:00-17:00, Sun 09:00-17:00; shops open daily 10:00-19:00.*

■ **PETTICOAT LANE** ✳   **25 D3**
A crowded and characterful market for clothes, jewellery and other goods. *Open Sun 09:00-14:00 in Middlesex Street and adjacent.*

■ **PORTOBELLO ROAD** ✳   Outside **26 A1/2**
Famous for the cosmopolitan atmosphere of its Saturday market, antiques predominate but there are also clothes, silver, china and more. *Open Sat 08:00-16:00.* From Mon-Fri there is a general market. ● *Ladbroke Grove, Notting Hill Gate.*

Specialist Shopping

■ **DENMARK STREET**   **30 A1**
A series of shops offering new and pre-owned musical instruments of all kinds along with associated accessories and services.

■ **HATTON GARDEN**   **23 D3**
This street and the adjacent area is the nation's centre for gems, gold and silver jewellery.

■ **LONDON SILVER VAULTS**   **31 C1**
Shops housed in underground vaults, selling a vast quantity of antique and modern silverware.

■ **TOTTENHAM COURT ROAD**   **21 D2/3**
This long thoroughfare has numerous popular electrical and home furnishings stores.

PARKS & GARDENS

■ **CHELSEA PHYSIC**   Outside **36 A3**
GARDEN ✳
Founded in 1673 by the Society of Apothecaries of London, this botanical garden has more than 5,000 species. *Open Apr-Oct, Tue-Fri 11:00-18:00 (Jul-Aug Wed until 22:00), Sun 11:00-18:00; adult £9.90;* ☎ *020-7352 5646;* ● *Sloane Square.*

■ **GREEN PARK**   **29 C3**
Some 53 acres made a royal park by Charles II.

■ **GREENWICH PARK** ✳✳   **44**
The oldest enclosed royal park and the only one east of central London. Within the 183 acres one finds several historic buildings, most notably the **Royal Observatory**✳✳ (see page 7).

■ **HYDE PARK** ✳✳✳   **28 A3**
  & KENSINGTON GARDENS ✳✳   **26 B2**
Of the parks in central London, Hyde Park (350 acres) is the most popular and, together with Kensington Gardens (275 acres) it forms the largest continuous space in London where one can easily forget that this is the centre of a bustling city. On the lake, called the **Serpentine** in Hyde Park and **Long Water** within Kensington Gardens, it is possible to row and swim in the summer. **Rotten Row**, on the south side, is a famous sandy track reserved for horse riding. The **Serpentine Gallery** and **Sackler Gallery** *(see page 13)*, in Kensington Gardens, hold contemporary art exhibitions.

■ **REGENT'S PARK** ✳✳✳✳   **20 A1**
With an area of 410 acres, this is the largest and one of the prettiest parks in central London.

It was laid out from 1812 onwards by John Nash for the Prince Regent, along with Regent Street and Portland Place, as part of a processional route connecting the park with the Prince's palace, Carlton House (demolished in 1829), in The Mall. It is bordered on three sides by classical **terraces**✳✳, designed by Nash and his disciple Decimus Burton. Each of these terraces has an imposing façade in the style now known as Regency.

Inside the park lies the beautiful expansive boating lake and, at its centre, **Queen Mary's Gardens**✳✳, considered to be London's most beautiful public grounds, with one of the nation's best rose gardens. On the north side of these gardens lies the **Open Air Theatre** which was founded in 1932 and opens from June to August, usually showing plays by Shakespeare, musicals, concerts and children's theatre.

■ **ROYAL BOTANIC**   Outside the map
  GARDENS (Kew Gardens) ✳✳✳✳
This is one of the world's finest botanic gardens. *Open daily from 09:30 and closing time varies according to the season; adult £15, free for under-17s;* ☎ *020-8332 5655;* ● *Kew Gardens.*

■ **ST. JAMES'S PARK** ✳✳✳   **38 A1**
This 58 acre area is one of the most beautiful of the royal parks and dates back to the 16th century. It was remodelled by John Nash (1829) who created the lake which is now full of ducks, pelicans and geese. To the north of the park is **The Mall**✳✳, the wide processional way from Buckingham Palace to Whitehall.

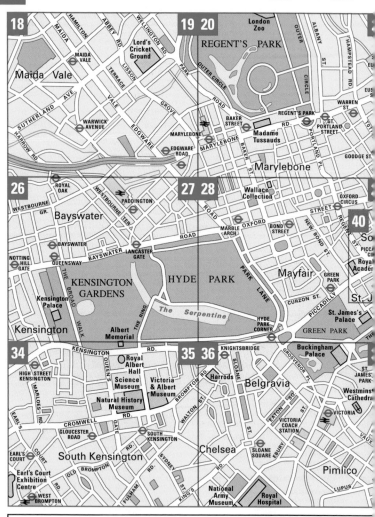

18 — Maida Vale

MAIDA VALE · Lord's Cricket Ground · WARWICK AVENUE

19 20 — REGENT'S PARK · London Zoo

BAKER STREET · Madame Tussauds · REGENT'S PARK · GT. PORTLAND STREET · WARREN ST · GOODGE ST. · EDGWARE ROAD · MARYLEBONE · Marylebone

26 — ROYAL OAK · PADDINGTON · Bayswater · BAYSWATER · QUEENSWAY · NOTTING HILL GATE

27 28 — Wallace Collection · OXFORD CIRCUS · MARBLE ARCH · OXFORD · BOND STREET · NEW BOND ST. · Mayfair · GREEN PARK · CURZON ST. · PICCADILLY · HYDE PARK CORNER

KENSINGTON GARDENS · HYDE PARK · The Serpentine · Kensington Palace · Albert Memorial · Kensington · THE BROAD WALK · THE RING · PARK LANE

40 — So... · PICCA... CI... · Royal Academy · St. J... · St. James's Palace · GREEN PARK

34 — HIGH STREET KENSINGTON · Royal Albert Hall · Science Museum · Natural History Museum · CROMWELL RD. · GLOUCESTER ROAD · SOUTH KENSINGTON · South Kensington · EARL'S COURT · Earl's Court Exhibition Centre · WEST BROMPTON · MARLOES RD · EARL'S RD

35 36 — KNIGHTSBRIDGE · Harrods · Victoria & Albert Museum · Belgravia · Chelsea · SLOANE SQUARE · National Army Museum · Royal Hospital · KING'S RD · FULHAM RD · WALTON ST · SLOANE ST · Buckingham Palace · ST. JAMES'S PARK · Westminster Cathedral · VICTORIA · VICTORIA COACH STATION · EATON SQ · Pimlico · LUPUS · VAUX...

KEY TO SYMBOLS on pages 18 to 41 & 44

- Place of interest
- Park, green space
- Rail or coach station
- Hospital
- Selected shop
- Pedestrian or paved area
- Elevated walkway
- Street or indoor market
- Road with bus services
- Overground railway line
- Vehicle through-way restricted
- No vehicle throughway
- Public access restricted
- Underground station
- Docklands Light Railway station
- Main National Rail station
- Other National Rail station
- River Trip Services

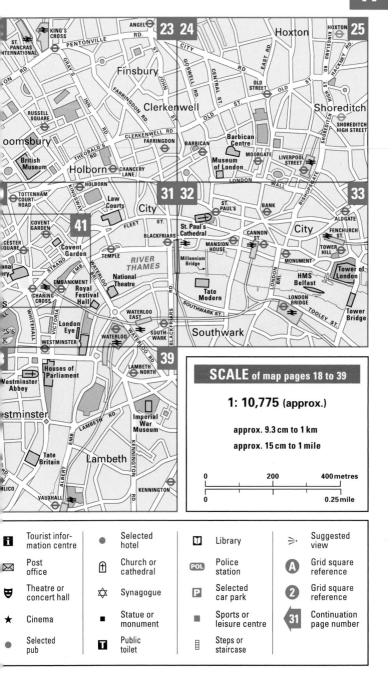

SCALE of map pages 18 to 39

1 : 10,775 (approx.)

approx. 9.3 cm to 1 km

approx. 15 cm to 1 mile

0	200	400 metres

0		0.25 mile

🅸	Tourist information centre	●	Selected hotel	📖	Library	≽·	Suggested view
✉	Post office	✝	Church or cathedral	POL	Police station	Ⓐ	Grid square reference
😃	Theatre or concert hall	✡	Synagogue	P	Selected car park	❷	Grid square reference
★	Cinema	■	Statue or monument	■	Sports or leisure centre	31	Continuation page number
●	Selected pub	🚻	Public toilet	▤	Steps or staircase		

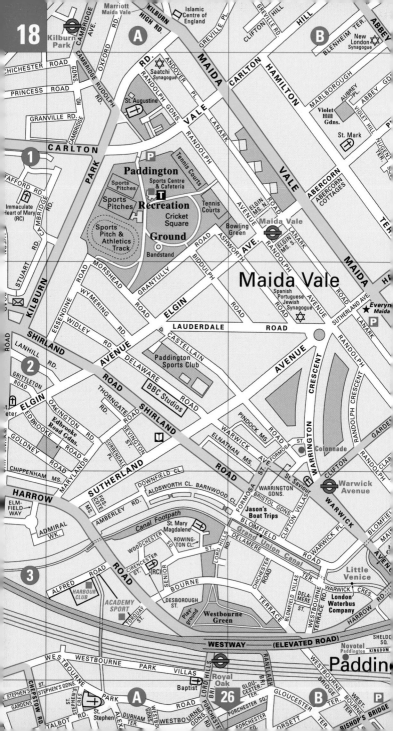

Marriott Maida Vale
Islamic Centre of England

A

B

Kilburn Park

New London Synagogue

CHICHESTER ROAD

PRINCESS ROAD

GRANVILLE RD.

STAFFORD RD.

CAMBRIDGE AVE.
OXFORD RD.
CAMBRIDGE GDNS.
RUDOLPH RD.

KILBURN HIGH RD.

GREVILLE PL.

CLIFTON RD.

GRANVILLE RD.

GRANVILLE HILL

BLENHEIM TER.

ABBEY

MAIDA VALE

CARLTON HILL

HAMILTON

Saatchi Synagogue
St. Augustine

RANDOLPH PL.
ANDOVER PL.

MARLBOROUGH
AUBREY PL.
ABBEY GDNS.

Violet Hill Gdns.

St. Mark

VIOLET HILL RD.

1

CARLTON

PARK

KILBURN

STUART RD.

Immaculate Heart of Mary (RC)

P

Paddington

Sports Pitches

Sports Pitches

Recreation

Sports Pitch & Athletics Track

Cricket Square

Ground

Bandstand

Sports Centre & Cafeteria

Tennis Courts

Tennis Courts

Bowling Green

RANDOLPH AVENUE

ELGIN MS. N.
ELGIN MS. S.

Maida Vale

LANARK RD.

LANARK MS. S.

RANDOLPH AVENUE

ABERCORN

ABERCORN COTTAGES

MAIDA

HA

MORSHEAD ROAD
WYMERING RD.
ESSENDINE ROAD
WIDLEY RD.

GRANTULLY ROAD

BIDDULPH ROAD

ASHWORTH ROAD

Maida Vale

Spanish Portuguese Jewish Synagogue

SUTHERLAND AVE.

Everyn Maida

P

ROAD

SHIRLAND

LANHILL RD.

2

GRITTLETON ROAD

ELGIN

eter

EDBROOKE

AVENUE

ROAD

DELAWARE ROAD

LAUDERDALE ROAD

CASTELLAIN ROAD

Paddington Sports Club

ROAD

AVENUE

CRESCENT

RANDOLPH CRESCENT

RANDOLPH

GARDE

OAKINGTON RD.
THORNGATE RD.
SEVINGTON ST.

BBC Studios

SHIRLAND

SUTHERLAND PL.

ROAD

PINDOCK MS.

WARWICK AVE.

ELNATHAN MS.

FORMOSA ST.

Colonnade

CLIFTON

RANDOLPH

CLAP

GOLDNEY ROAD
EDBROOKE ROAD

CHIPPENHAM MS.

MARYLANDS RD.

SUTHERLAND

ROAD

DOWNFIELD CL.

ALDSWORTH CL. BARNWOOD CL.

WARRINGTON GDNS.

BRISTOL GDNS.

St. Saviour

WARRINGTON

CLIFTON PL.

Warwick Avenue

HARROW

ELM-FIELD WAY

ADMIRAL WK.

POST MS.

AMBERLEY RD.

Canal Footpath

FORMOSA ST.

CLIFTON VILLAS

WARWICK

BLOMFIE

MAIDA

3

ROAD

ALFRED ROAD

HARBOUR CLUB

ACADEMY SPORT

TORQUAY ST.

WOODCHESTER ST.

CIRENCESTER ST.

SENIOR ST.

St. Mary Magdalene

ROWINGTON CL.

(RC)

LORD HILLS RD.

Grand Union Canal

DELAMERE ROAD

Jason's Boat Trips

BLOMFIELD ROAD

WARRINGTON

CHICHESTER ROAD

CLIFTON VILLAS

BLOMFIELD VILLAS

DELA-MERE TER.

BLOMFIELD TERRACE

WARWICK PL.

Little Venice

London Waterbus Company

WARWICK CRES.

HARROW RD.

AVENU

BOURNE ROAD

DESBOROUGH ST.

Play-ground

Westbourne Green

WESTBOURNE TERRACE

WESTWAY (ELEVATED ROAD)

Novotel Paddington

SHELDO SQ.

KINGDOM

Padding

WESTBOURNE PARK VILLAS

Royal Oak

26

LORD HILLS RD.

RANELAGH BRI.
GLOU-CESTER TER.
BRI.

WESTBOURNE BRIDGE

P

A

STEPHEN'S GDNS.
ST. STEPHEN'S CRES.
GARDENS

CHEPSTOW RD.

Baptist

ROAD

DURHAM TER.

ALEX.

St. Stephen

TALBOT RD.

WESTBOURNE PARK ROAD

PORCHESTER TER.

GLOUCESTER TER.

B

DORSETT TER.

PORCHESTER SQ.

PORCHESTER SQ.

BISHOP'S BRIDGE

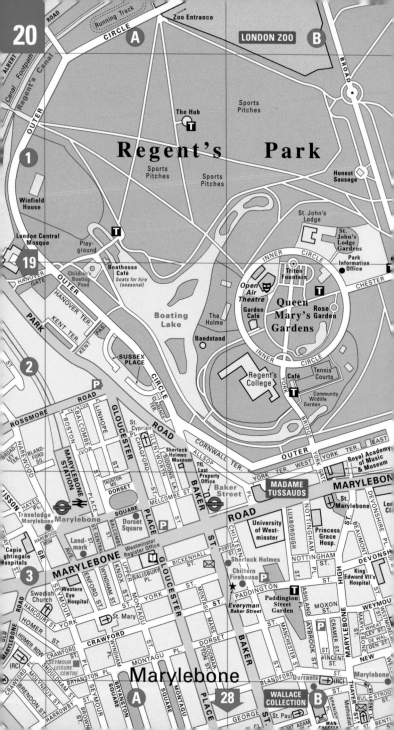

ROAD

CIRCLE

A

Running Track

Zoo Entrance

B

BROAD

Canal · Footpath

Regent's Canal

ALBERT

OUTER

The Hub
T

Sports
Pitches

1

Regent's   Park

Sports
Pitches

Sports
Pitches

Honest
Sausage

Winfield
House

St. John's
Lodge

London Central
Mosque

Playground

T

St. John's
Lodge
Gardens

Park
Information
Office

T

HANOVER
GATE

19

OUTER

HANOVER TER.

Children's
Boating
Pond

Boathouse
Café
boats for hire
(seasonal)

INNER   CIRCLE

Triton
Fountain

CHESTER

PARK

KENT TER.

KENT PAS.

Boating
Lake

Open
Air
Theatre

Garden
Café

Queen
Mary's
Gardens

Rose
Garden

T

ST.

2

SUSSEX
PLACE

The
Holme

Bandstand

T

INNER   CIRCLE

Café

Tennis
Courts

ROSSMORE

ROAD

CIRCLE

Regent's
College

YORK

T

Community
Wildlife
Garden

P

TAUNTON
PL.

BALCOMBE ST.

LINHOPE
ST.

CHAGFORD
ST.

St.
Cyprian
Pl.

GLENTWORTH
ST.

BRIDGE

OUTER

EAST

BROAD
LEY
TER.

HARE-
WOOD
ROW

BLAND-
FORD SQ.

BOSTON
PL.

IVOR
PL.

GLOUCESTER
PL.

SIDDONS LA.

Sherlock
Holmes
Museum

CORNWALL TER.

ALLSOP
PL.

YORK TER. WEST

YORK
GATE

YORK TER.

Royal Academy
of Music
& Museum

MARYLEBONE

TISSON

HAYES
PL.

MARYLEBONE STATION

Travelodge
Marylebone

Marylebone

TAUNTON
PL.

DORSET
ST.

MELCOMBE ST.

SQUARE

BAKER
ST.

Baker
Street

**MADAME
TUSSAUDS**

PL.

MARYLEBONE

St.
Marylebone

Lor
Cl

DEVONSHIRE PL.

TWAY

Capio
ghtingale
hospitals

3

Swedish
Church

Western
Eye
Hospital

Land-
mark

HARE-
WOOD
ROW

CENTRAL

AVE.

BALCOMBE
ST.

ENFORD ST.

KNOX
ST.

UPPER

WYNDHAM ST.

Westminster
Register Office

SALISBURY
PL.

YORK

MARYLEBONE

P

Dorset
Square

GLOUCESTER
PLACE

BICKENHALL
ST.

MONTAGU
ST.

CHILTERN ST.

PORTER ST.

Sherlock
Holmes

Chiltern
Firehouse

ROAD

University
of West-
minster

PADDINGTON

Paddington
Street
Garden

LUXBOROUGH
ST.

NOTTINGHAM
PL.

NOTTINGHAM
ST.

Princess
Grace Hosp.

DEVONSH

BEAUMONT ST.

King
Edward VII's
Hospital

WEYMOU

HIGH

OLD
MARYLEBONE
ROAD

HOMER
ROW

HOMER
ST.

HARCOURT ST.

SEYMOUR PL.

St. Mary

CRAWFORD
PL.

CRAWFORD
ST.

WYNDHAM
PL.

MONTAGU
PL.

MONTAGU
MANS.

MONTAGU
ST.

DORSET
ST.

BAKER
ST.

T

Everyman
Baker Street

Paddington
Street
Garden

P

MANCHESTER
ST.

ASHLAND

AYBROOK ST.

MOXON
ST.

CRAMER
ST.

ST.
VINCENT
ST.

MARYLEBONE

NEW

MOXLYNEUX
ST.

(RC)

SHOUTHAM ST.

BRYANSTON
PL.

BRYANSTON
SQUARE

Marylebone

A

MONTAGU
SQUARE

SEYMOUR LEISURE
CENTRE

BRENDON
ST.

HARROWBY
ST.

BROWN
ST.

CRAWFORD
ST.

GLOUCESTER
PLACE

BLANDFORD
ST.

Durrants

(RC)

**WALLACE
COLLECTION**

GEORGE
ST.

St. Paul

SPANISH PL.

THAYER
ST.

MAN-
CHESTER

ST. ADAM

WEL

BUL
MER

BENTI

Methodist

28

B

Marylebone

WEYMOUTH ST.

DE WAL

LEY

WHEAT
CL.

MARYLEBONE

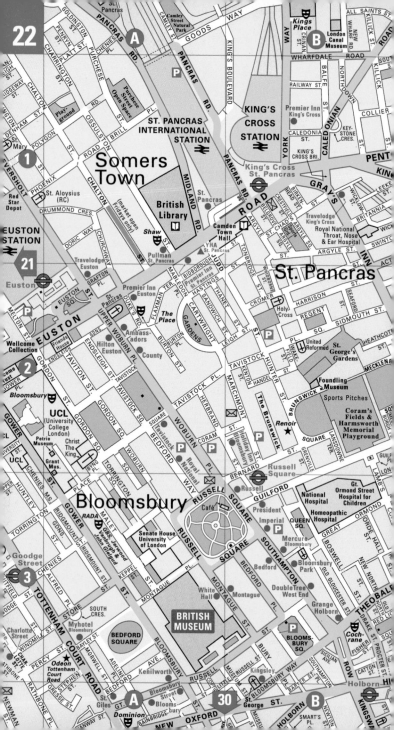

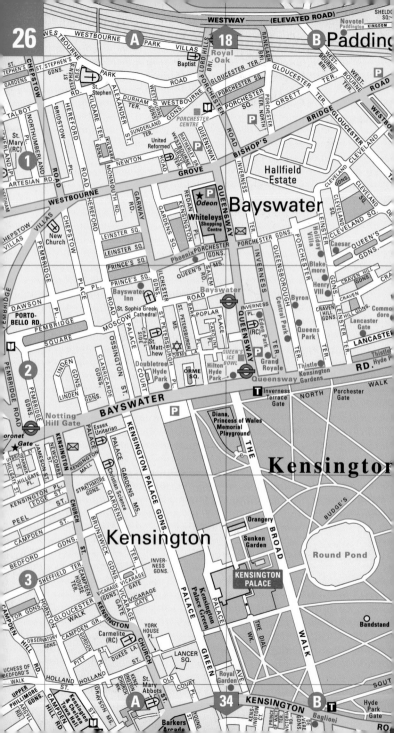

WESTWAY (ELEVATED ROAD)

SHELDO SQ.

Novotel Paddington KINGDOM

WESTBOURNE PARK

VILLAS

18

Royal Oak

B Padding

St. STEPHEN'S GARDENS

ST. STEPHEN'S RD.

WESTBOURNE PARK

Baptist

GLOUCESTER TER.

PORCHESTER SQ.

GLOUCESTER SQ.

WEST BOURNE BRI.

WEST BOURNE

ROAD

TALBOT RD.

St. Stephen

DURHAM TER.

WESTBOURNE GDNS.

PORCHESTER TER. NORTH

ORSETT

PORCHESTER TER.

BRIDGE

GLOUCESTER TER.

CLEVELAND TER.

CHEPSTOW

NORTHUMBERLAND PL.

HEREFORD ROAD

BRIDSTOW PL.

KILDARE GDNS.

ST.

KILDARE TER.

SUNDERLAND TER.

PORCHESTER CENTRE

QUEENSWAY

BISHOP'S

Hallfield Estate

CLEVELAND

CLEVELAND GDNS.

CLEVELAND SQ.

WESTBO

St. Mary (RC)

1

United Reformed

MATHERYUR.

WESTBOURNE GDNS.

INVERNESS

ARTESIAN RD.

WESTBOURNE

HEREFORD

GARWAY

ROAD

NEWTON RD.

MONMOUTH RD.

GROVE

KENSINGTON

REDAN

Odeon

Whiteleys Shopping Centre

Bayswater

PORCHESTER GDNS.

LEINSTER GDNS.

CLEVELAND SQ.

QUEEN'S

HEPSTOW VILLAS

New Church

CHEPSTOW VILLAS

LEINSTER SQ.

LEINSTER SQ.

PRINCE'S SQ.

GARWAY RD.

PHOENIX

PORCHESTER GDNS. MS.

QUEEN'S

PORCHESTER GDNS.

INVERNESS TER.

LEINSTER GDNS.

QUEENSBOROUGH TER.

Holiday Villa

Caesar

QUEEN'S GDNS.

CRA

PEMBRIDGE PLACE

ULCHESTER GDNS.

PRINCE'S SQ.

SALEM

Blake more

PORCHESTER TER.

CRAVEN HILL GDNS.

CRAVEN

Commo dore

EMBRIDGE

DAWSON PL.

PEMBRIDGE PL.

Bayswater Inn

St. Sophia Greek Cathedral

MOSCOW ROAD

ST. PETERSBURGH MS.

POPLAR PLACE

Bayswater

INVERNESS PL.

Byron

Henry VIII

QUEENSBOROUGH TER.

CRAVEN HILL GDNS.

CRAVEN HILL

Lancaster Gate

PORTO-BELLO RD.

PEMBRIDGE SQUARE

OSSINGTON ST.

CLANRICARDE GDNS.

St. Matthew

ST. PETERSBURGH PL.

CHAPEL

CAROLINE

Eden Park

QUEENSWAY

Queens Park

LANCASTE

2

LINDEN GDNS.

LINDEN

Doubletree Hyde Park

ORME SQ.

ORME LA.

Queen's ICE BOWL

Hilton Hyde Park

Grand Royale

Thistle

Kensington Gardens

Thistle

RD. Hyde P

Notting Hill Gate

BAYSWATER

P

Queensway

Inverness Terrace Gate

NORTH

Porchester Gate

WALK

oronet Gate

Essex Unitarian

KENSINGTON PALACE GARDENS

PALACE

Diana, Princess of Wales Memorial Playground

THE

Porchester Gate

UXBRIDGE SIDRAMMER

NEWCOMBE

Kensington MALL

PALACE GARDENS

Christian Science

BROAD

Kensington

HILLGATE ST.

HILLGATE PL.

STRATHMORE GDNS.

KENSINGTON GARDENS MS.

Kensington

Orangery

Sunken Garden

KENSINGTON PL.

EDGE ST.

BRUNSWICK GDNS.

PEEL ST.

CAMPDEN GDNS.

BEDFORD GDNS.

INVER-NESS GDNS.

KENSINGTON PALACE

Round Pond

3

SHEFFIELD TER.

CAMPDEN HOUSE TER.

VICARAGE GATE

VICARAGE GATE

Kensington Palace Green

BUDGE'S

Bandstand

TOR GDNS.

HORNTON ST.

VICARAGE GDNS.

VICARAGE GATE

York House PL.

PALACE

THE DIAL

OBSERVATORY GDNS.

CAMPDEN GR.

ST.

CAMPDEN ST.

KENSINGTON CHURCH ST.

Carmelite (RC)

DUKES LA.

LANCER SQ.

GREEN

WALK

CAMPDEN HILL RD.

UCHESS OF BEDFORD'S WALK

PITT ST.

OLD COURT

Royal Garden

HOLLAND

HOLLAND ST.

DRAYSON MS.

A

KENSINGTON CHURCH WK.

St. Mary Abbots

34

KENSINGTON

B

T

Hyde Park Gate

PHILLIMORE GDNS.

ARGYLL RD.

CAMPDEN HILL RD.

Kensington Town Hall

KENS.INGTON CT.

PRINCE OF WALES

DE VERE GDNS.

Baglioni

SOUT

Barkers Arcade

YOUNG ST.

RO

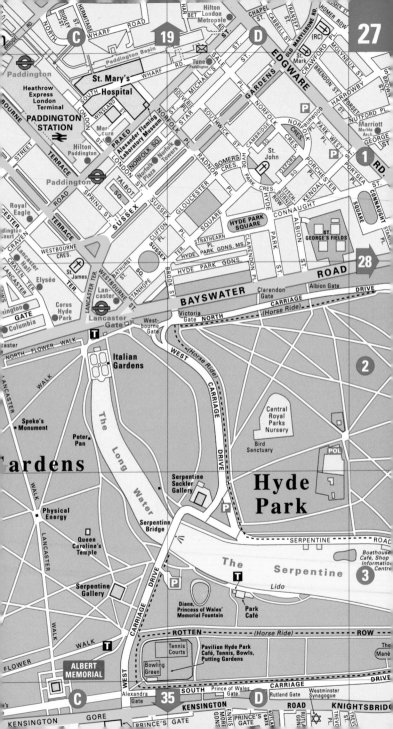

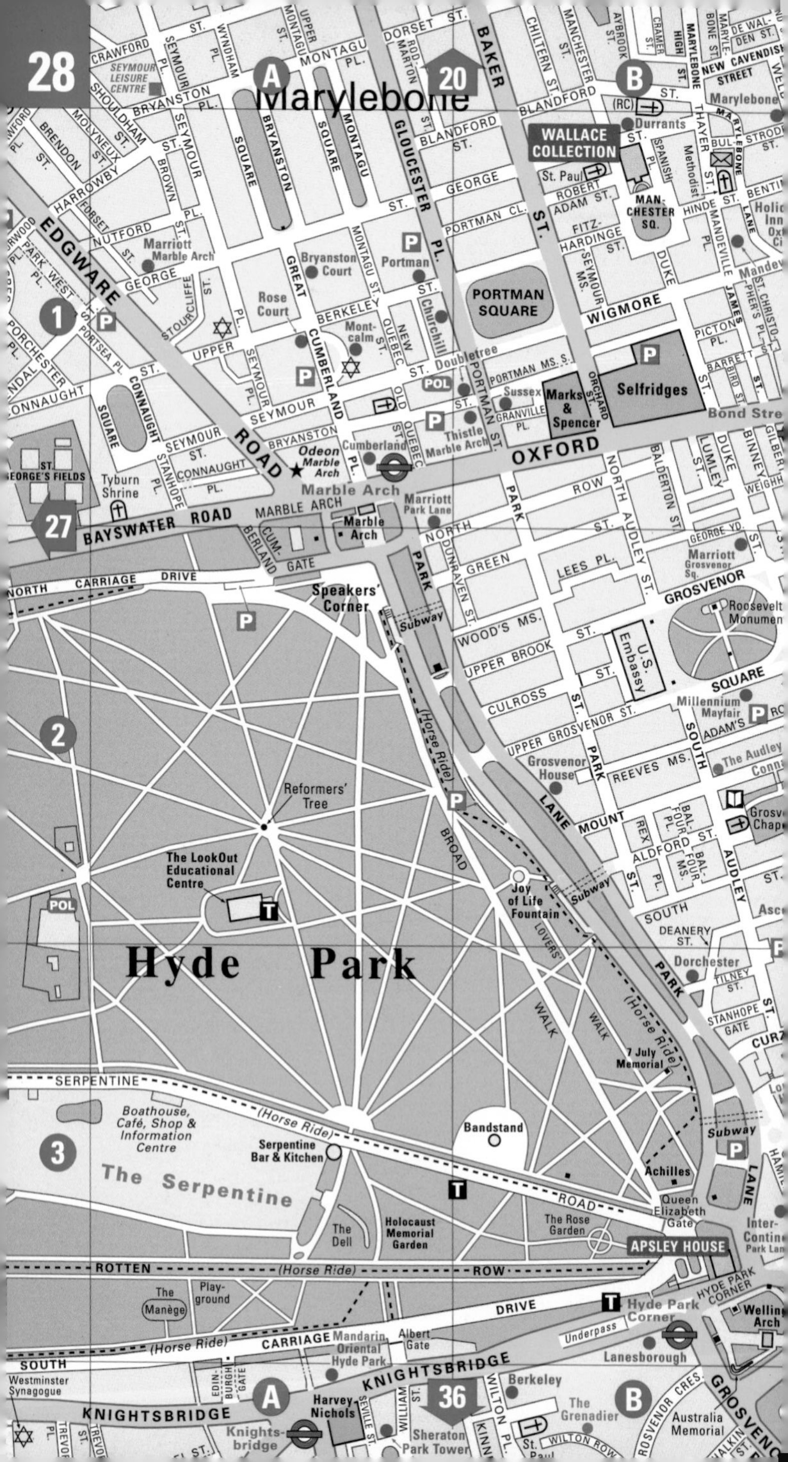

A 20 B

CRAWFORD ST.
SEYMOUR LEISURE CENTRE
BRYANSTON PL.
UPPER MONTAGU ST.
MONTAGU ST.
MONTAGU PL.
DORSET ST.
BAKER ST.
CHILTERN ST.
MANCHESTER ST.
AYBROOK ST.
CRAMER ST.
MARYLEBONE HIGH ST.
NEW CAVENDISH ST.
DE WALDEN ST.
WEL...

SHOULDHAM ST.
WYNDHAM PL.
SEYMOUR PL.
BRYANSTON SQUARE
BLANDFORD ST.
(RC)
DORSET ST.
MANCHESTER SQ.
ST. VINCENT ST.
Marylebone
Methodist
Durrants
THAYER ST.
MARYLEBONE LANE
Hollis ...
Oxf... Ci...

BRENDON ST.
MOLYNEUX ST.
NUTFORD PL.
BROWN ST.
MONTAGU SQUARE
GEORGE ST.
BLANDFORD ST.
WALLACE COLLECTION
St. Paul's
ROBERT ADAM ST.
SPANISH PL.
MAN-CHESTER SQ.
HINDE ST.
BENTI...

HARROWBY ST.
NUTFORD PL.
Marriott Marble Arch
GREAT CUMBERLAND PL.
MONTAGU MS. W.
PORTMAN CL.
GEORGE ST.
PORTMAN SQUARE
FITZ-HARDINGE ST.
SEYMOUR MS.
DUKE ST.
JAMES ST.
PICTON PL.
Marie ...
GILBE...

EDGWARE ROAD
1
P
PORCHESTER PL.
PARK WEST
Rose Court
Bryanston Court
Berkeley Court
Portman
Montcalm
Doubletree
Sussex
Granville PL.
Marks & Spencer
Selfridges
WIGMORE ST.
ORCHARD ST.
BINNEY ST.
LUMLEY ST.
Bond Stre...

CONNAUGHT SQUARE
STOURCLIFFE ST.
UPPER BERKELEY ST.
SEYMOUR ST.
NEW QUEBEC ST.
ST. DOUBLETREE
OLD QUEBEC ST.
PORTMAN MS. S.
PORTMAN ST.
Thistle
POL
St. Michael
Cumberland
Odeon Marble Arch
BALDERTON ST.
DUKE ST.

SEYMOUR ST.
BRYANSTON ST.
Marble Arch
Thistle Marble Arch
OXFORD ST.
NORTH AUDLEY ST.
GROSVENOR ST.

ST. GEORGE'S FIELDS
Tyburn Shrine
STANHOPE PL.
SEYMOUR ST.
CONNAUGHT ST.
27
BAYSWATER ROAD
Marble Arch
MARBLE ARCH
CUMBERLAND GATE
Marble Arch
Marriott Park Lane
NORTH ROW
LEES PL.
GEORGE YD.
Marriott Grosvenor Sq.
GROSVENOR SQUARE

NORTH CARRIAGE DRIVE
Speakers' Corner
Subway
WOOD'S MS.
UPPER BROOK ST.
U.S. Embassy
Roosevelt Monument
Roosevelt ...

GREEN PARK
DUNRAVEN ST.
PARK LANE
CULROSS ST.
UPPER GROSVENOR ST.
Millennium Mayfair
ADAM'S ...
2
Reformers' Tree
The LookOut Educational Centre
T
(Horse Ride)
Grosvenor House
REEVES MS.
The Audley
Conn...
Grosv... Chape...

POL
Joy of Life Fountain
Subway
MOUNT ST.
BAL-FOUR PL.
REX PL.
ALDFORD ST.
BAL-FOUR MS.
AUDLEY ST.
Asce...

Hyde Park
SOUTH
DEANERY ST.
Dorchester
TILNEY ST.
STANHOPE GATE
F...

BROAD WALK
7 July Memorial
Subway
CUR...

SERPENTINE
(Horse Ride)
Boathouse, Café, Shop & Information Centre
Serpentine Bar & Kitchen
Bandstand
Achilles
LOVERS WALK
WALK
(Horse Ride)
PARK LANE
Subway
P
3
The Serpentine
The Dell
Holocaust Memorial Garden
Serpentine Road
The Rose Garden
Queen Elizabeth Gate
APSLEY HOUSE
Inter-Contine... Park Lane

ROTTEN
(Horse Ride)
ROW
DRIVE
T
Hyde Park Corner
Welling...

The Manège
Play-ground
CARRIAGE
(Horse Ride)
Underpass
Lanesborough
HYDE PARK CORNER
Hyde Park Arch

SOUTH
Westminster Synagogue
EDIN-BURGH GATE
Mandarin Oriental Hyde Park
Albert Gate
A
Harvey Nichols
36
KNIGHTSBRIDGE
WILTON PL.
Berkeley
WILTON ROW
The Grenadier
B
ROSVENOR CRES.
GROSVENOR
Australia Memorial

KNIGHTSBRIDGE
Knightsbridge
Sheraton Park Tower
WILTON ST.
ST. WILTON ROW
...WALKIN...

BBC

All Souls

C **21** **D** **1** SOHO SQ.

HARLEY

DUCHESS

MANSFIELD

PORTLAND PL.

LANGHAM

RIDING HOUSE ST.

GREAT

WELLS

NASSAU

CHARLOTTE

Rathbone

PERCY

Charlotte Street

WINDMILL

RATHBONE

NEWMAN ST.

RATHBONE PL.

Langham

St. Georges

MORTIMER

LITTLE PORTLAND

CHFIELD

All Saints

Sanderson

BERNERS ST.

GRESSE ST.

ANNE

WIGMORE

QUEEN ANNE MS.

CHANDOS ST.

CAVENDISH PL.

PORTLAND

GARET

MARKET PLACE

Welsh Baptist

EASTCASTLE

WELLS ST.

The Plaza

London Edition

WARDOUR

DEAN

French Ch.

Totter Court

CAVENDISH STREET

HOLLES ST.

House of Fraser

SQUARE

MAR-GARET ST.

CASTLE ST.

WINSLEY ST.

BERWICK

Totter ST.

St. Peter

BHS

John Lewis

PRINCE'S

OXFORD

OXFORD

ST.

YHA Oxford Street

HOLLEN

ST. ANNE'S

ROYALTY MS.

MEARD ST.

FRITH

enhams

ST.

Oxford Circus

Marks & Spencer

RAMILLIES

NOEL D'ARBLAY

Soho

HENRIETTA

VERE ST.

SWALLOW PAS.

ARGYLL

London Palladium

HILLS PL.

Photographers' Gallery

BROADWICK

WARDOUR

BERWICK

HOPKINS ST.

INGESTRE

St. MARTINS

Berkshire

NEW

HAREWOOD PL.

PRINCES ST.

REGENT

GT. MARLBOROUGH

FOU-BERT'S PL.

Liberty

MARSHALL ST. LEISURE CENTRE

LEXINGTON

OLD ADWICK

HANOVER SQ.

HANOVER ST.

POLLEN ST.

Jaeger

CARNABY

KINGLY ST.

DAVIES L.

SOUTH MOLTON LA.

Handel House Mus.

ST. GEORGE ST.

St. George

Hamleys

ST.

BRIDLE LA.

BREWER

DENMAN ST.

SHAFTESBURY AVE.

Fenwick

MADDOX ST.

NEW BURLINGTON ST.

TENISON WAY

BEAK ST.

GOLDEN SQ.

Ripley's Believe It Or Not!

Trocadero

BROOK'S MS.

Claridge's

Sotheby's

AVERY ROW

CONDUIT

Wesbury

BOYLE ST.

SAVILE ROW

(RC)

WARWICK

SHERWOOD

GLASSHOUSE ST.

COVENTRY

SVENOR

GROSVENOR HILL

BOND

CLIFFORD ST.

Burberry

CORK ST.

Burberry

VIGO ST.

Austin Reed

Piccadilly Circus

REGENT

ST.

HAYMARKET

BOURDON

BRUTON PL.

GRATTON ST.

Asprey

ST.

BURLINGTON GDNS.

SACKVILLE ST.

2

JERMYN

ST. ALBAN'S

BERKELEY SQUARE

BRUTON LANE

Garrard

ALBEMARLE

BURLINGTON ARC.

ROYAL ACADEMY OF ARTS

PICCADILLY

PRINCE'S ARC.

St. James

DUKE OF YORK ST.

ST. JAMES'S

CHARLES II

Mayfair

HAY HILL

DOVER ST.

Browns

OLD BOND ST.

PICCADILLY ARC.

Fortnum & Mason

DUKE ST. ST. JAMES'S

ST. JAMES'S SQ.

Duke of York's Column

CHESTERFIELD

CHARLES

FITZ-MAURICE PL.

Fleming Collection

STAFFORD ST.

Holiday Inn Mayfair

JERMYN

St. James

St. James's

CLEVE LAND

CARLTON GDNS.

CARLTON H.

QUEEN ST.

Washington

May Fair

BERKELEY STREET

BOLTON ST.

Green Park

Ritz

ARLINGTON ST.

Christie's

KING

PALL

RAC

Crewe House

Flemings

HALF MOON ST.

Green Park

Stafford

ST. JAMES'S PL.

RIDER

Marlborough House

CARLTON

MALL

Shepherd Market

ST.

Dukes

ST. JAMES'S STREET

Gatehouse

CROWN PASS.

3

Christ Ch.

Park Lane

PICCADILLY

QUEEN'S

Spencer House

CLEVELAND ROW

Queen's Chapel

MALL

Four Seasons

Hard Rock Cafe & The Vault

Athenaeum

Green Park

ST. JAMES'S PALACE

Clarence House

(Closed to traffic on Sundays)

Summer Bandstand

Lancaster House

THE

St. James's Park Lake

Canada Memorial

WALK

D St. **St. James's Park**

CONSTITUTION (Horse Ride) HILL

(Closed to traffic on Sundays)

Queen Victoria Memorial

Commonwealth Memorial

C **37**

Buckingham Palace Gardens

BUCKINGHAM PALACE

The Quadrangle

The Forecourt

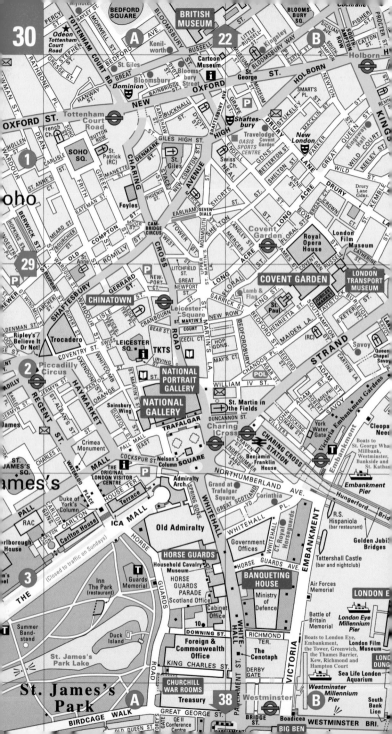

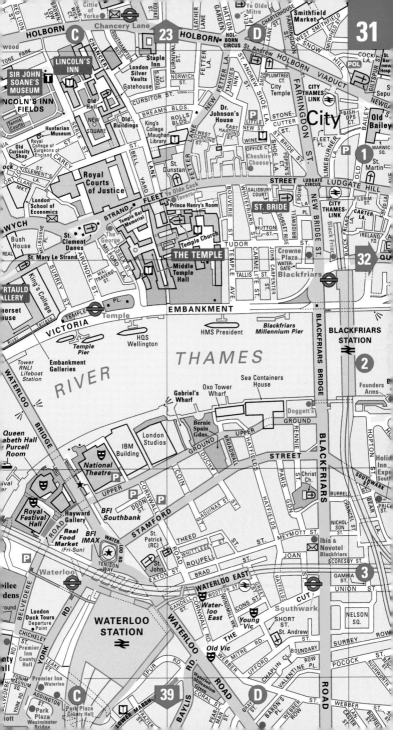

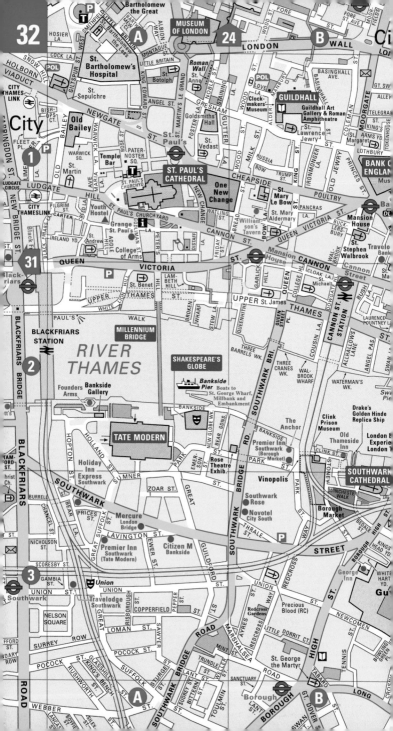

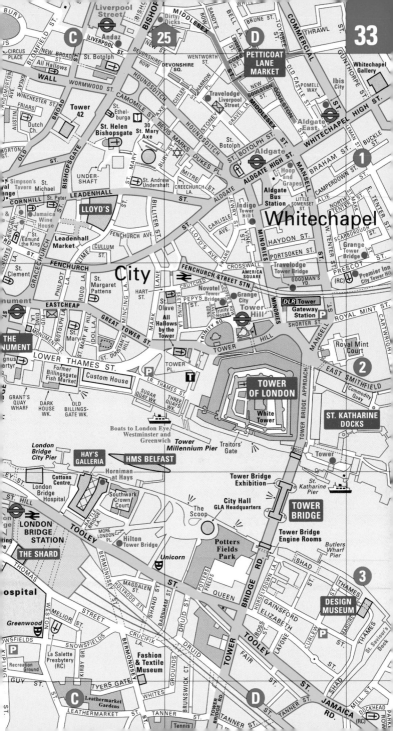

Whitechapel

City

TOWER OF LONDON

White Tower

TOWER BRIDGE

THE SHARD

LONDON BRIDGE STATION

HMS BELFAST

HAY'S GALLERIA

ST. KATHARINE DOCKS

PETTICOAT LANE MARKET

LLOYD'S

THE MONUMENT

DESIGN MUSEUM

Potters Fields Park

Liverpool Street

Whitechapel Gallery

Ibis City

Aldgate East

Tower Bridge
Exhibition

Tower Bridge
Engine Rooms

City Hall
GLA Headquarters

The Scoop

Fashion
& Textile
Museum

Carmelite (RC)
DUKES LA.
LANCER SQ.
PALACE GREEN
PALACE AVE.
KENSINGTON CHURCH ST.
BROAD WK.

P. PHILLIMORE
HOLLAND
GORDON PL.
PITT ST.
HORNTON ST.
HOLLAND ST.
DRAYSON MEWS
St. Mary Abbots
OLD COURT PL.
YOUNG ST.
KENSINGTON
Royal Garden
Palace Gate
Baglioni
Hyde Park Gate
SOUT...
HYDE PARK GATE

CAMPDEN HILL ARGYLL PL.
HILLIMORE PL.
ESSEX VILLAS
STAFFORD TER.
IMORE GARD.
HORNTON ST.
KENSINGTON CHURCH WK.
Linley Sambourne House
PHILLIMORE WALK
ADAM AND EVE MS.
HIGH
Barkers Arcade
Marks & Spencer
High Street Kensington
KENSINGTON
SQUARE
THACKERAY ST.
PRINCE OF WALES TER.
KENSINGTON CT.
DE VERE GDNS.
PALACE GATE
HYDE PARK GATE
KENSINGTON

KENSINGTON
ALLEN ST.
WRIGHTS LA.
IVERNA COURT
IVERNA GDNS.
Christian Science
St. Sarkis Armenian Church
ADAM AND EVE MS.
CHENISTON GDNS.
MARLOES
SOUTH END ROW
ST. ALBAN'S GR.
DOURO PL.
CANNING PL.
VICTORIA GR.
ALBERT PL.
GATE
QUEEN'S GATE
KENSINGTON GATE
QUEEN'S G
PETERSHAM

Our Lady of Victories (RC)
ABINGDON
PATER ST.
COPE PL.
United Reform
SCARSDALE VILLAS
Kensington Close
Copthorne Tara
SCARSDALE PL.
KELSO PL.
ST. MARGARETS LA.
STANFORD ROAD
COTTESMORE GDNS.
ELDON RD.
Christ Church
VICTORIA
KYNANCE PL.
KYNANCE MS.
ELVASTON
GATE

RLS WK.
PEMBROKE SQUARE
IMORE PL.
ABINGDON VILLAS
Coptic
STRATFORD ROAD
ST. MARY'S GATE
CHANTRY SQ.
ST. MARY'S
CORNWALL GDNS.
CORNWALL GDNS.
GRENVILLE PL.
SOUTHWELL GDNS.
QUEEN'S GATE GDNS.
Strathmore
Rydges

PEMBROKE ROAD
EARL'S COURT ROAD
St. Philip
LEXHAM MS.
RADLEY MS.
LEXHAM GARDENS
LEXHAM
LEXHAM GDNS.
Mercure Kensington
PENNANT MS.
Parkcity
Sainsbury's Superstore
EMPEROR'S GATE
St. Stephen
Crowne Plaza
Vand
Montana
S

LOGAN PLACE
MacOwan
WEST CROMWELL ROAD
Cromwell Hospital
NH Kensington
CROMWELL
KNARESBOROUGH PL.
CROMWELL RD.
Easy-Hotel
Kensington Rooms
Ashburn
Holiday Inn Kens. Forum
CROMWELL
Gloucester Road
GLOUCESTER ROAD
REDFIELD LANE
Park Grand
Marriott Kensington
Ambassadors
Park Int.
ASHBURN GDNS.
RD. Bailey's
COURTFIELD
Gloucester
GDNS.

EARL'S
KENWAY RD.
TEMPLETON PL.
WALLGRAVE RD.
HOGARTH RD.
Enterprise
Indigo Kensington
COLLINGHAM PL.
COLLINGHAM GDNS.
COURTFIELD GDNS.
COURTFIELD
St. Jude's
COURTFIELD RD.
Bentley
HARRINGTON GDNS.
COLBECK MS.
HARRINGTON
WETHERBY GDNS.
Harrington Hall
ROSARY GDNS.

NEVERN PL.
LONGRIDGE RD.
SPEAR MS.
NEVERN ROAD
Burns
EARL'S COURT GDNS.
BARKSTON GDNS.
HESPER MS.
BRAMHAM GDNS.
LAVERTON PL.
COLLINGHAM RD.
WETHERBY
BOLTON GDNS.
GLEDHOW GDNS.
BINA GDNS.
Cranley
DRAYTON

NEVERN SQ.
George
TREBOVIR RD.
EARL'S COURT
Earl's Court
Earl's Court
PENYWERN RD.
Garden View
WARWICK
HILBEACH GDNS.
Earl's Court
EARL'S COURT RD.
BARKSTON GDNS.
BRAMHAM GDNS.
BOLTON GDNS.
YHA Earl's Ct.
ROAD
THE BOLTONS
St. Mary
CRESSWELL PLACE
ROAD

EARL'S COURT EXHIBITION CENTRE
EARDLEY CRES.
KEMPSFORD GDNS.
EARL'S COURT ROAD
OLD BROMPTON ROAD
WARWICK RD.
COLEHERNE RD.
WHARFE DALE ST.
REDCLIFFE SQ.
FINBOROUGH RD.
St. Luke's
REDCLIFFE GDNS.
HARCOURT TER.
THE BOLTONS
THE LITTLE BOLTONS
BOLTONS PL.
REDCLIFFE
GILSTO

ibis Earl's Court
LILLIE ROAD
OLGA ST.
BRICKETT ST.
SEAGRAVE RD.
Lily
West Brompton
FINBOROUGH RD.
COLEHERNE RD.
REDCLIFFE MS.
WESTGATE TER.
REDCLIFFE RD.
FINBOROUGH RD.
FINBOROUGH RD.
GARDENS
HOLLYWOOD RD.
HOLLYWOOD RD.
WESTGATE TER.
TREGUNTER RD.
CATHCART RD.
SEYMOUR
REDCLIFFE RD.

West Brompton
Open Air
Brompton Cemetery

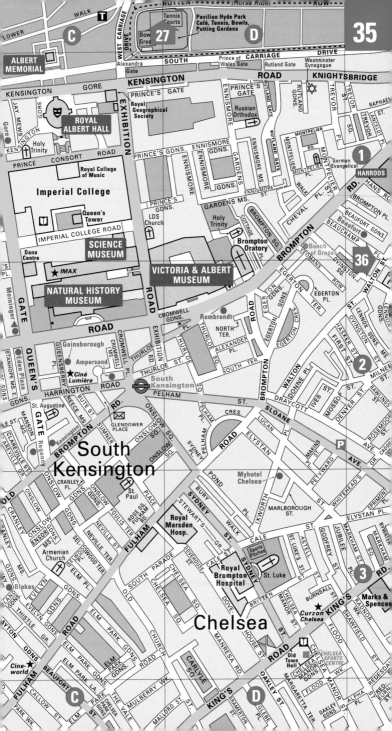

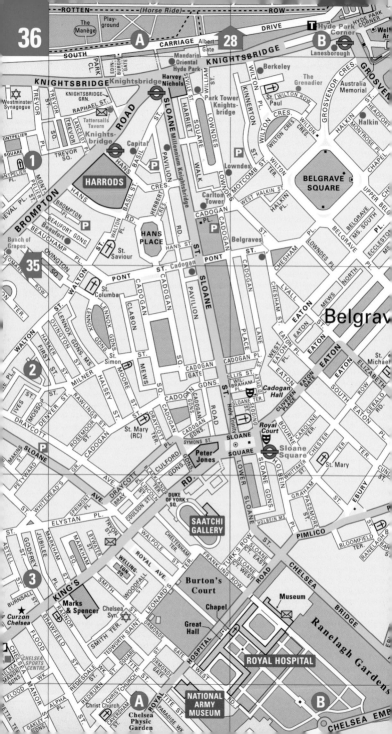

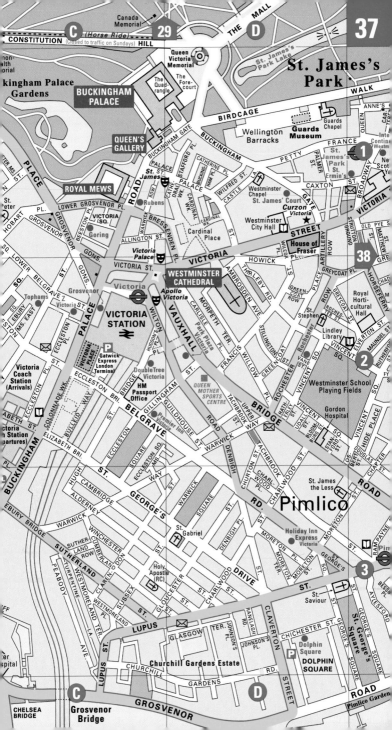

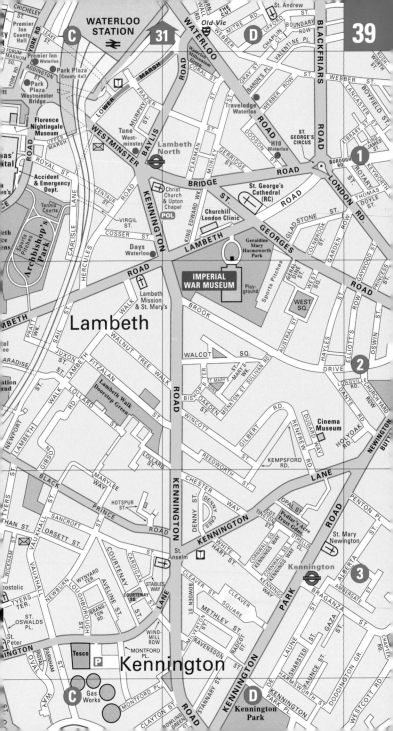

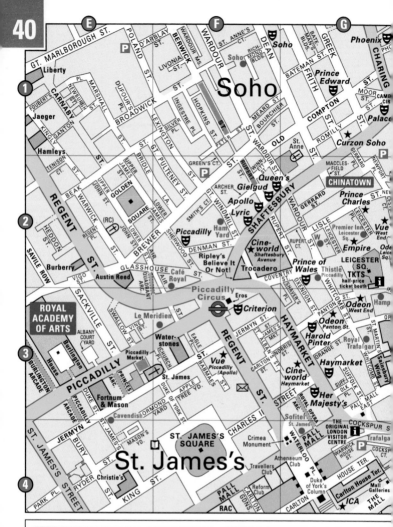

TIPS FOR THEATREGOERS

To discover details of what is on at London's theatres, look out for the free fortnightly *London Theatre Guide* at theatres, hotels and tourist information centres in central London. In addition, go to *www.officiallondontheatre.co.uk* for the latest information.

TKTS (half-price theatre ticket booth)
Situated in the clocktower building on the south side of Leicester Square *(see map square G2 above)*, this shop is run by the official *Society of London Theatre* and offers discounted and half-price tickets for same day performances. *Open Mon-Sat 10:00-19:00, Sun 11:00-16:30; due to high demand, early queuing is advisable.*

MAIN THEATRES & CONCERT HALLS